PRAISE FOR

THE CREATIVE CALL

"To be an artist, receiving the vision and applying creativity may not be enough. Janice Elsheimer models, and suggests to the reader, many of the practical ways of living the fruitful artist's life. Packed with lived-out illustrations of what it takes in the way of discipline and daily dedication to respond to God's creative call, this book blesses and illuminates."

—LUCI SHAW, poet and author of *The Angles of Light, Water My Soul,* and *Friends for the Journey* (with Madeleine L'Engle)

"Janice Elsheimer's book will be an invaluable aid for artists in all fields, helping the creative person get closer to the source of true creativity."

—BRYAN SAVAGE, best-selling saxophonist and flutist whose albums include *Cat Food, Soul Temptation,* and *Rush Hour*

"*The Creative Call* will reawaken and embolden artists to take responsibility for naming, developing, and expressing their creative gifts. The exercises here have the potential to transform an artist's understanding of who God originally created him or her to be, and to provide courage and discipline to actually produce work! I highly recommend that groups of artists work through this material in the context of community, to encourage and challenge one another."

—NANCY BEACH, programming director and teaching pastor at Willow Creek Community Church

"Human creativity has been like a prodigal longing to return to its father. Janice Elsheimer guides the artist home."

—ERWIN RAPHAEL MCMANUS, lead pastor of Mosaic, artist, futurist, and author of *An Unstoppable Force*

"I wish I'd had Janice Elsheimer's inspiring and spirit-filled book over twenty years ago when I first started writing. *The Creative Call* speaks to all of us—the professional artist who is already making a living at an art form, as well as the beginning writer, dancer, poet, photographer who is unsure whether he or she even has the right to be called an artist. Most importantly, Elsheimer reminds all of us that God fashioned us to be creative beings. *The Creative Call* is a book that I will return to time and time again."

—JOYCE HANSEN, author of numerous books including
I Thought My Soul Would Rise and Fly and *Breaking Ground, Breaking Silence*

"*The Creative Call* acknowledges the tug of war that takes place within the heart of every creative Christian—the tug between the desire to be an artist and the weight of responsibility that is felt when it is ignored. Janice Elsheimer affirms the artist's desire to follow his or her own creative call and to be true to the Holy Spirit."

—BECKY ANN LAMB, author of *God's Precious Gift in a Manger*

"This is an extraordinarily inspiring book that I sprinkled with exclamation marks as it revealed my heart of hearts. It drew me from inertia to a place of life."

—KAREN HANSON, director of women's ministry
at Northland Church, Florida

"When I worked through *The Creative Call,* I experienced both an artistic and spiritual revival. My artwork has changed, and I'm actively producing art and encouraging other artists to speak with their artwork as a voice for Christ among other voices presented in the art world."

—PHYLLIS THOMAS, watercolor/mixed-media artist
and parachurch art ministry coordinator

"Following *The Creative Call* made me realize that my creative spirit was not being given free reign. I'm thankful to Janice for listening to God's creative call in her own life and sharing her vision with us."

—REV. SARAH H. GAEDE, Orlando, Florida

THE CREATIVE CALL

A WRITERS' PALETTE BOOK

An Artist's Response to the Way of the Spirit

THE CREATIVE CALL

Janice Elsheimer

WATERBROOK
PRESS

The Creative Call

PUBLISHED BY WATERBROOK PRESS

12265 Oracle Boulevard, Suite 200

Colorado Springs, Colorado 80921

ISBN: 978-0-87788-138-4

Published in the United States by WaterBrook Multnomah, an imprint of the Crown Publishing Group, a division of Random House Inc., New York.

WATERBROOK and its deer colophon are registered trademarks of Random House Inc.

Printed in the United States of America

2012

11 10 9

To my son, James,
my husband, Seth, and my mother, Phyllis:

Your love lights my way.

Contents

FOREWORD

So many times I've heard someone admire another's talent and longingly say, "I used to be able to do that!" My follow-up question is always, "Why did you stop?" People come up with a myriad of answers to that question but often they come to the sad realization that they never really had to stop. I frequently catch a glimpse of the sense of fulfillment they once enjoyed—now long gone, but not forgotten.

The unfortunate truth is that once we have found our way in the so-called "real world," even if we become successful in a chosen profession, many of us discover we've lost something of ourselves. We lose the simple pleasure that we once cherished of being who God created us to be and doing what God created us to do. We may even feel our gifts are lost forever. But are they?

In *The Creative Call,* Janice Elsheimer lays out steps to reawakening the artist inside us. This practical guide helps us examine the circumstances that led to the abandoning of our precious talents in the first place and offers us the keys to unlocking the unique treasure we still have buried deep within.

As Janice points out, a number of stumbling blocks may have hindered the development of our artistic selves. We may have encountered unbelief in the benefits of our special gifting. Too many times, after someone has enjoyed viewing my own artwork, I've been told, "You know, my child (or niece, nephew, friend, or whoever it may be) showed a talent for art, but then they finally wised up and got a 'real job.'" This comment is like fingernails on a blackboard to me! Unfortunately, many people have this misconception. Somewhere along the way, people equated certain talents, especially the arts, with laziness or foolishness. But in truth, artistic and creative thinkers have helped shape our society! It is this truth that is important to hold on to as we develop our art.

Another stumbling block is our own fear. Many of us may have felt that we just weren't good enough to be an artist. But I ask, "Not good enough for whom?" I learned a long time ago that no matter how good you are there will always be somebody better. So I stopped worrying about how good I was compared to others and simply concentrated on becoming the best that I could be. We become good at our gift by using our talents—by exercising our creative muscles and developing skills, confidence, and an understanding of our craft.

Chapter by chapter, with thought-provoking words and exercises, Janice lifts the veil that blinds our thoughts towards our gifts. Most of us will be able to see ourselves somewhere within the pages of this book. We will then have the chance to overcome the lies that have kept us from believing that we can enjoy the wonderment of creating with the talent we possess.

Wonderful journeys begin with the first step. Janice helps us begin to pull off the weights that hinder our talents and learn to seek the Holy Spirit's guidance to regain a belief in pursuing our gifts. As our trust level develops, she encourages us to go on to the next step—just do it! Step by step we make our way toward the threshold of a newly resurrected talent. This journey is not so much about where we are going, but what we're doing to get there.

Nothing will take the place of working at our craft. That is why it's important not to become frustrated when our skill level doesn't match our expectations. It takes time to reacquaint ourselves with our reawakened talent. Instead of expecting perfection, we should expect to make mistakes and learn from them—to use them as a part of our personal growth process. To my knowledge, no masterpiece was ever created during the first attempts to grow familiar with a particular medium. If we learn to enjoy the developmental process and not be afraid to make mistakes, eventually we'll learn the truth of the craft. True excitement comes when we realize that the more we exercise our gift the more joy and satisfaction we feel and the more skilled we become. It's all a part of the journey. So, we might as well enjoy it!

—THOMAS BLACKSHEAR, illustrator, painter, and creator of the limited edition prints,
"Forgiven," "Coat of Many Colors," "Lord of All," and "Watchers in the Night"

Preface

I try to avoid using words like *God-ordained*. Such jargon, particular to Christian writers and believers, carries connotations that can put others off. This type of parlance confuses the language of spirituality. Language should edify and unify, not separate and stratify. In the case of this book, however, I just can't seem to get around it: writing *The Creative Call* was a God-ordained appointment, an offer I couldn't refuse.

This book grew out of a need that surfaced during a twelve-week study of *The Artist's Way* by Julia Cameron, a bestseller in the field of creativity that deals with artistic development as a spiritual issue. The opportunity to participate in this study group came at a time when I was ready to start paying more attention to my own artistic talents, and I hoped that Cameron's book would stimulate the sleeping artist within me. It did, and I am sincerely grateful to Ms. Cameron. Her groundbreaking work in this area initiated my own creative revival.

The group I was in was comprised of Christians. Since Cameron's book seemed to focus more on finding oneself through practicing one's art than on practicing one's art in order to discover a deeper relationship with God, a week did not pass without someone saying, "If only we could find a book like this for Christians." I felt that wish as a deep calling. I put aside other writing projects and began to write *The Creative Call*.

My research led me to many writers who had thought and written a great deal about Christians as artists and their responsibilities to their talents, to God, and to the world. I immersed myself in works, both Christian and secular, on the subject of creativity and artistic development. But I never found what the people in my group were looking for: a biblically-based book designed to teach the reader how to reawaken the artist within and how to use art as a pathway to a closer walk with God. *The Creative Call* is the product of my own creative reawakening. May the reading of it be as much of a blessing in your life as the writing of it has been in mine.

ACKNOWLEDGMENTS

Years ago, after she read my first Christmas newsletter, my good friend Marilynda Farris called from Arkansas to tell me I should be a writer—that in fact I was a writer and just needed to do something about it. Marilynda will always be among my heroes for believing in me long before I knew how to believe in myself as an artist.

This book would not exist in its present form had it not been for the encouragement and assistance of the people in my first artists' group at Orlando Community Church. Steve Andrews, Dave Capp, John and Nancy Christiansen, Judy English, Ted Greenberg, Peggy Homrich, Jackie Hughes, Trisha Martin, Janice Morgan, Phyllis Thomas, Dawn Ogden, and Norm Veldon helped tremendously in the birthing of this book. Their enthusiasm and diligent evaluation of the course and their pointing out the book's strengths and weaknesses was invaluable.

I also want to thank my first group of practicing artists from Northland Community Church for their insights and encouragement: Val Garber, Esther Horvath, Nina Snyder, and Kaye Hannah, along with my ever-faithful Phyllis Thomas, who has been my friend and encourager since the book's inception and who taught the course for me before the book went to press. Without the assurance that it could truly make a difference in how readers felt about their art and their relationship with God, I would have never allowed this book to be published.

I am grateful to the people who served as my extra eyes, not only in copyediting the text, but also in offering wonderful suggestions for tightening up the style and format. Thanks to Jackie Hughes for her interest, her hours of work, and her friendship through all the frustration and joy of creating this book. Heartfelt appreciation goes to my "brother-in-love" Greg T. Smith, whose comments and suggestions were both insightful and entertaining. Elizabeth Swanson's honest and encouraging non-Christian appraisal of the manuscript was invaluable. Finally, the book you have in your hands would not exist had it not been for the sensitive intelligence and keen eyes of my editor, Elisa Fryling, and my production editor, Laura Wright.

My friend John Christiansen, pastor of Orlando Community Church, deserves special recognition for his encouragement and his words of wisdom throughout the writing and testing of this book. His admonition to believe that this project was not so much about getting published as about doing God's will helped me get out of the way and let the Holy Spirit do his work.

Finally, to my best friend and best love, my husband Seth Elsheimer: Thank you for calling me a writer before I could bring myself to use the word and for believing that, in writing this book, I was following my own creative call.

Always give yourselves fully to the work of the Lord,
because you know that your labor in the Lord is not in vain.

—1 Corinthians 15:58

WONDERING

When I was young I found a kind of salvation in two forms of creative expression: writing and playing the piano. From the time I was seven or eight years old, I kept diaries and poured into them all the wondering and confusion of childhood and adolescence. Teachers and parents said I had a gift for writing and a talent for music, and even as a child I felt that these gifts were from God, that they were not just something he gave *to* me but something that came *through* me. When the music seemed to move beyond me, or when my writing produced just the right effect, I felt uplifted, light, complete.

PLAYING BY HEART

I recall memorizing Beethoven's "Für Elise" for a recital when I was nine. That hauntingly beautiful music taught me why learning a piece by memory was called learning it *by heart:* Only after I had committed a piece to memory was I free to explore the emotions elicited by the music. Until I knew a piece by heart, I could not put expression into it, expression that came from my heart, that breathed life into the notes and turned my playing from an exercise to an art. I often wondered how my friends who didn't have music or writing in their lives handled *their* deep feelings. What did they do "by heart"?

Years later, however, when I began to make college and career decisions, it didn't occur to me to major in English, journalism, or musical performance, even though these were the areas of my greatest talents. I decided on music education after being advised that very few women pianists had ever risen to the top in the world of musical performance. Teaching was the only sure way to make a living with music. Caution and fear of failure kept me from believing I could become a professional musician. It did not occur to me at that time to ask God to reveal his vision for my life. On my own, following my head rather than my heart, I chose the safe path.

In my sophomore year I switched my major to English education, still choosing to teach what I loved to *do:* read and write. I discarded thoughts of majoring in pure English or journalism as too risky. What I thought I wanted most (besides to change the world and to get us out of Vietnam) was to become financially secure. Even though my father has a great deal of artistic ability, eternal optimism, and an entrepreneurial spirit, he never tried to make a living as an artist. Still, he demonstrated often enough that risk taking can result in a life of financial uncertainty. I might not get rich teaching, I reasoned, but at least I would have job security.

At the age of twenty-three I embarked on a career as an educator that allowed me to teach every grade level from elementary school through college. I enjoy a sense of pride and satisfaction when I reflect on those years of using my creativity and love of language to touch the lives of so many others. Still, no matter how successful a teacher I may have been, I always had a feeling God wanted more from me. Maybe, I began to think, he wanted me to quit hiding the light of my talents under the basket of security I had woven for myself. Maybe I needed to start letting those talents shine beyond the comfortable confines of my study and my music room. Thoughts like that led me to start teaching part time and to begin spending some serious, focused time on becoming a writer.

"To whom much is given, from him much will be required" (Luke 12:48, NKJV). Creative people know that not only are they missing something important when they aren't exercising their creative gifts, but they are also shrinking from the responsibility they have to develop those gifts. In the years in which the piano sat untouched and the only writing I did was when I wrote letters, journal entries, or comments on my students' essays, I experienced a nagging sense of sadness and, yes, *guilt*. And although this book is not about acting on our talents out of guilt, I believe there is a reason many of us feel guilty when we aren't practicing our art. If God has given us the gift of creativity, "much is required" in the way of our using it to his glory.

GIFTS THROUGH US

Our gifts are not from God to us, but from God through us to the world. When we fail to use these gifts, we suffer the same way a person accustomed to regular physical activity may feel pent up, out of sorts, and off-balance after going for several days without exercise. When we try to live without exercising our artistic gifts, we may feel restless and empty. Life lacks fullness. Something buried deep within longs to emerge.

Job wrote, "For I am full of words, and the spirit within me compels me; inside I am like bottled-up wine, like new wineskins ready to burst. I must speak and find relief; I must open my lips and reply" (Job 32:18-20). If we have neglected to develop and use the talents God has given us, we feel incomplete, unfulfilled, unfinished, even depressed. We are "like new wineskins ready to burst." We devour books, we travel, we acquire possessions, or we busy ourselves in relationships and careers. We engage in diversions of all kinds in an attempt to find that elusive thing called *fulfillment*. We spend our time and money in a fruitless search to "find ourselves" instead of finding out how God wants us to use the talents he has given us.

I believe that creatively gifted people spend a disproportionate amount of time and money in psychotherapy because they haven't spent enough time practicing their art. Although the healing value of counseling should not be underestimated, sooner or later, once we've done all the work of looking into the past and trying to understand how we arrived where we are in life, we inevitably come face to face with ourselves and with God. In the end we come to know this: We can't do a thing about the past, but to some extent we can and do have control over the present.

That's what this book is about. No matter how busy, overworked, or under pressure you may be, if you have a sincere desire to use the gifts God has given you and if you are willing to do your part, God will be faithful to do his. As the lessons of this book unfold, you will discover that "your part" is to honor and develop the artist within you. "God's part" is to help you find the time and resources to do that and to use what you create to his glory.

> *Our vocation is not simply to be, but to work together with God in the creation of our own life, our own identity, our own destiny.*
>
> —THOMAS MERTON

You may be reading this because you have been burying your talents and you are ready to get serious about unearthing them. Perhaps you suspect you have artistic talents, but you have never had the opportunity to develop them. Maybe you've set your art aside for the sake of family or career. Lack of time, energy, or confidence might be the culprit. You may even be an artist who has used your gifts to develop a successful career but you're tired of producing what the market demands rather than following your own creative inclinations. Maybe others, believing they're looking out for your best interests, have cautioned you to the point of undermining your confidence. Perhaps you have always thought it was just too arrogant to believe you have talent worth sharing. If any of these statements resonates with you, then it's time to dig down deep and see what lies beneath the surface of your life. It may be time to discover what you have missed by not finding the time, the energy, or the confidence to use the gifts God has given you to express what's in your heart.

This book is about reclaiming God's vision for us as his artists. "Perseverance must finish its work so that you may be mature and complete, not lacking anything" (James 1:4). This book is about choosing a new way to live and then persevering until we are whole, mature, and complete people.

WHY THIS BOOK?

Other books have been written for those who want to recommit to using their creative gifts. Some of these books encourage the reader to focus on some vague Creative Source or one's Higher Power to pursue art through spiritual renewal. They even apologize if their use of the word *God* sounds "too Christian." These authors recognize that practicing one's art is a spiritual matter, but they tend to dance around the issue of who God is and who we are in relation to him. *It's okay to talk about spirituality,* they seem to say, *as long as we aren't too specific about who or what the source of that spirituality is.* This position appeals to those who wish to define the spiritual world in a comfortably ambiguous way: God becomes synonymous with Self, a nebulous force of Nature, or a form of Creative Energy.

Most artists see creativity and spiritual growth as intimately related, but Christian artists go a step further. They understand the need to reconnect our talents back to their source: the God who created us and who calls us to become a cocreator with him. *The Creative Call* offers Christians a point of view and an approach that is consistent with Christ's teachings. Instead of hoping that finding ourselves will result in practicing our art again, we need to realize that only through *losing* ourselves and becoming reliant on God can we discover how to use those gifts the way he wants us to use them. We will find the artist God intends us to be when we empty ourselves of *self* and become open to his plan and to the inspiration of his Holy Spirit. Only then will we experience personal artistic revival.

ANSWERING THE CREATIVE CALL

I wrote this book to help artistic Christians reclaim their vision of themselves as artists. The chapters have been set up to allow the reader to work through the book a week at a time at a fairly leisurely pace. No pressure, no guilt.

This design works for either individuals or groups. I have led numerous groups of aspiring and practicing artists (from musicians and actors to gourmet cooks and gardeners) through *The Creative Call*. Many people enjoy the group discussions, the accountability that comes from doing a book with a group, and the emotional and prayer support of the other group members. Jesus said in Matthew 18:20 (RSV), "For where two or three are gathered in my name, there am I in the midst of them." Working with a group helps some of us find deeper unity with God and other artists as we experience artistic renewal in a supportive, communal environment.

But you may choose to go through the book on your own, making your study a private and contemplative communion with God and with your artistic self. Some people who have read the book alone later pulled together a group of people to form a small *Creative Call* group. It's wonderful to have one person who has already done the book on his or her own lead a group of people who wish to work through the book together.

Beginning with chapter 2, each chapter includes five exercises. (I have put just a few exercises in chapter 1 so that if you are doing the book as a group, you can work through chapter 1 together at your first meeting, completing the exercises as you go.) Whether you go through the book on your own or in a group, I suggest you take a chapter a week, breaking each one down into about five readings. From chapter 2 on, you may want to read the material leading up to and including one exercise each day, allowing you two days off each week. You don't have to complete any of the exercises, but I expect that you will want to since they contain the real work of the course. If you meet with a discussion group, part of each meeting will involve sharing what you've thought about and discovered during the previous week. You will probably want to read parts of your responses to the rest of the group. Doing so is a good way to invite the group's input as you process your creative development. Sharing responses can also encourage you as you discover that others in your group are experiencing many of the same feelings you are. If you are working alone you will still benefit from the insights you'll receive by doing the exercises.

Most of the exercises can be done right in the book. Sometimes you will want to use an exercise as a prompt for writing in your *artist's daybook,* a journal you will keep as you spend these eight weeks reawakening the sleeping artist within you. You will write in this daybook for twenty minutes each day. I will be discussing the rationale for journaling in chapter 2, but feel free to begin your artist's daybook right away if you wish. The purpose of the daybook is threefold. It will encourage you to keep a record of this journey you are beginning. It will also help you set aside a specific time each day to listen to what God has to reveal to you about yourself and your art. Finally, it will help you develop the habit of participating in at least one creative activity every day, which is an important step in becoming a more productive artist.

> *When I'm operating at my best, my work is my prayer. It comes out of the same place that prayer comes out of—the center, the heart.*
> —MATTHEW FOX, PH.D.

Each chapter begins with a verse of scripture that you should try to memorize. Learning the verse will impress on your mind the theme of the chapter. I find that practicing the "memory verse" throughout the week keeps me more tuned in to what God has to say to me through that scripture as I go about this creative-awakening work. If you are studying *The Creative Call* with others, you might want to take turns reciting the memory verse at the beginning of each meeting.

You will find as you go through the book that one of the keys to unlocking your creativity is action: *simply doing the next thing that needs to be done.* Picking up this book is an example of this kind of "affirmative action." If you are willing to give about an hour's attention each day, five days a week, to applying the lessons of this book, at the end of eight weeks you will see a difference in how you look at your gifts, how you use your time, and how you view yourself as an artist. You will:

- learn to call on the Holy Spirit as your source of inspiration, your muse.
- exercise your artistic gift regularly and begin to think of yourself as an artist.
- develop the habit of journaling as a way to recognize the things that have kept you blocked.
- have a richer, deeper prayer life and a more intimate relationship with Jesus Christ.

Whatever your talent, if you are ready for God to reveal his vision for your life as one of his artists, if you are ready to bring that talent into the light where the Holy Spirit can infuse you with the breath of heaven—if you are ready to start playing by heart—read on.

CHAPTER ONE

BEGINNING

In the beginning was the Word, and the Word was with God,
and the Word was God. He was with God in the beginning. Through him all things
were made; without him nothing was made that has been made.

JOHN 1:1-3

I've always loved the image of Jesus as "the Word." The *Word,* through whom all things were made, is both the expression of God's creativity and God's own son, Jesus Christ. What a powerful image for artists who are just beginning to awaken their creativity: the Savior as the Word, through whom all things were made. Through the Word, the process of creation began. And through God's Word, our creative renewal will begin as well.

"Through him all things [we, our unique selves with our unique talents and abilities] were made." God has created us with our own artistic language—our "words" are the way we express ourselves creatively, regardless of our medium of expression. Whether you are seeking to discover or to reawaken the artist within you, the work you do in this book will bring to light your unique creative language, the artistic language that only you can speak through the power of the Holy Spirit and by his inspiration.

If we are to gain anything of value by uncovering our individual creativity, the discovery process first must bring us closer to our creative source, the "Word made flesh [who] dwelt among us." Our words, the expression of our art, will emerge as we place ourselves securely within the Word of God.

A NEW BEGINNING

This is a new beginning. As we begin the work of discovering or rediscovering our creativity, we should surround ourselves in prayers for protection and focus. The Artist's Creed below is a prayer you may want to use. (If you are using this book in a group setting, try reading it together using *we*.) As you work through the book, consider writing your own Artist's Creed to fit your personal vision of what you believe about being called to be one of God's artists.

If you have not done so already, stop now and pray for the guidance and wisdom of the Holy Spirit as you start this work of freeing the artist within you. You may want to use one of the prayers to the Holy Spirit in the appendix of prayers at the end of the book.

AN ARTIST'S CREED

I (we) believe my talents are a gift from God, and I am to use them to fulfill his purposes in my life and in his world. I humbly acknowledge and accept my gifts as I ask to receive God's vision for how I am to use them. I ask the Holy Spirit to free me from self-doubt and self-absorption. I pray this work will bring me into closer alignment with God's plan for me as I seek to bring my gifts and talents into his light and to become the whole and complete person he intends me to be. Amen.

WHAT IS AN ARTIST?

The *American Heritage College Dictionary* defines an artist as "one who creates imaginative works of aesthetic value." The second definition is "one whose work shows great creativity or skill." How do you define "artist"? Write your own definition on the lines below. *I think an artist is*

_____

_____

_____

The fine arts include visual, musical, theatrical, and literary creative production. The term *artist,* however, can also include the gourmet cook who creates marvelous culinary experiences, the gardener who uses nature as a palette, the photographer, the quilter, the potter, the weaver, the worker in stained glass, and anyone else who uses creativity to bring something new and meaningful into the world.

> *This, then, is the beginning: to know that we have a right to the creative and to follow it where it leads. Why should that be so difficult? We know things when we are very young that we forget as we age.*
> —DEENA METZGER

This book is written for people who feel they have an artistic talent and have buried it rather than developed it and for people who simply want to have a more meaningful artistic life. They feel that something has been missing in their lives. They want to either discover or more fully use their talents because they know that if they don't, they will be leaving something important undone.

You may be a person who is still looking for that medium through which to express yourself artistically, the medium in which your talents lie. Take heart in the fact that you are not alone. You are part of a renaissance that seems to be occurring throughout the adult population. My husband, a chemistry professor, discovered that he had a talent for acting when he was in his early thirties and has been performing in community theater ever since. In the past few years he has started translating his love of singing into working with several *a cappella* groups, sometimes even getting paid to perform. I recently gave him singing lessons as a birthday gift—the first music lessons he's ever taken. Never having had a music lesson or an art class when you were a kid is no reason to believe you don't have talent in those areas. So not only is this book addressed to people who have let their talents get rusty, it can also be useful to those who have always suspected that they have a talent but haven't yet begun to discover or develop it.

Try to Remember

Ask any group of young children if they are artists, and without hesitation they will tell you yes, they can draw, finger paint, make up songs, work in clay, dance, tell stories, and act in plays. Children are imaginative and creative by nature. "Can we draw a picture to go with our story?" is one of the most common questions I hear in the elementary school writing classes I teach. As we grow up, over time or sometimes quite suddenly, many of us stop exercising the talents that were once a natural and an important part of our life. Why does this happen?

Think back to when you were still using your talents or think about how you feel right now when you are using them. Become aware of how it feels to be involved in your art. Write three words or phrases describing how you feel when you allow your artist self to take over.

_____

_____

_____

What do these three words or phrases tell you about what creative activity once meant (or means) to you?

_____

_____

_____

Now think about how you feel when you are doing "adult," responsible things with your time. Write three words or phrases that describe how you feel when you are engaged in activities that don't involve your artist self.

_____

_____

_____

What does this exercise tell you about how you view these two sides of yourself?

_____

_____

_____

_____

Some people, recalling times when they were being creative, write words like *guilty, insecure, irresponsible, foolish, selfish, lonely,* or *"not good enough."* Others respond with words like *playful, carefree, daring, satisfied, fulfilled,* and *happy.*

When you think about your non-artist, grown-up life, words and phrases such as *responsible, trustworthy, dependable, financially secure, goal-oriented,* or *mature* might come to mind. Perhaps you wrote *frustrated, unhappy,* or *empty.* Whatever your responses, pay attention to what the words tell you about your attitude toward nurturing the artist within you.

The Fine Art of Intimidation

Life can intimidate the artist in you, and so can other people. And it is sometimes difficult to pin down the source of that intimidation. External intimidators, such as well-meaning parents, friends, teachers, or advisers who simply "wanted the best for you," may have encouraged you to pursue a "sensible" path rather than one that could have led to the full development of your talents. Maybe someone you admired when you were younger told you that you could never be a successful artist because they wanted to protect you from disappointment. A critical spirit within yourself, which compared your work with others' and found it wanting, may have been an internal intimidator. Perhaps just thinking about what it takes to get by financially in this world was enough to make you discard any thoughts about going into the arts as a career. Time and the busyness of life took care of the rest.

Ask yourself these questions: Have you actively sought God's will in this area of your life? Have you asked him what he wants you to do with the talents he has given you? Would you have made different decisions about your life had you sought and received a clear calling from God when you were younger? I believe that you can seek that appointment or anointing at any time in your life, even if you missed it as a young person.

The Bible recounts many examples of people who were called by God to do things that may have seemed unreasonable, or even irresponsible, to other people. Abraham's call to sacrifice his son, Moses' assignment to lead his people out of captivity, the dreams and visions of Jacob's son Joseph that took him to Egypt, exactly where God wanted to use him—these are just a few Old Testament examples. In the New Testament Jesus invited the disciples to leave their sensible, responsible lives for the chance to participate in the creation of something entirely new in the world. What if they, like the rich young man in the parable, had been unable to leave their worldly security behind and accept Jesus' invitation? And what about Jesus' mother, Mary? She was called to give birth to the Messiah, even though, as she points out to the angel Gabriel in Luke 1:34, she had not known a man. *There's* a calling that might have seemed irresponsible to some of her family members and friends!

Compared to these biblical figures, our calling as *artist* seems almost mundane—hardly daring or frightening at all. Yet when we get busy seeking our own path, setting our own goals, making our own plans, we often overlook or shy away from the very thing that could set us on the path toward spiritual fulfillment: seeking, hearing, and acting on God's vision for our life. This includes—maybe even especially includes—how we are to use our gifts and talents.

Instead of enjoying the creative life God intends for us to have, we may be spending a great deal of time and energy burying our talents so we won't be distracted from the sensible business of life—our careers, friendships, families; our school, church, social, and financial obligations. Without realizing it, we have wrapped up our imaginations and talents into neat little packages and stored them somewhere out of our range of consciousness. Paying attention to those important obligations in life is reasonable and responsible, and we'd be remiss if we didn't attend to them. But by not acknowledging that our gifts are a part of God's purpose for us, we stop exercising our playful, inventive, imaginative selves and instead focus only on the necessities of making a living, a home, a family, and a place for ourselves in the grown-up world.

In order to [create], you must face your inner critics, steal their power. Begin by trying to identify them.

—GEORGIA HEARD

Sometimes our closets, attics, and garages get so full of stuff that we no longer know what we have, and if we do, we no longer know where to find it. By the time we need something, it has been shoved so far behind our more current vintage possessions that we have to disassemble our entire closet, attic, or garage just to get to it. Similarly, when we bury our talents, we let more urgent activities and responsibilities pile up in front of our creative lives until the artist self is shoved to the back of the closet. Burying our talents is not something most of us have done on purpose; it is just something that gradually happens.

It is the creative potential itself in human beings that is the image of God.

—MARY DALY

Think about why you have buried your talent. Do you remember hearing or sensing the following "discouraging words" while you were growing up?

- "I'm just thinking of your future. Do you really want to spend your life struggling in as competitive a field as art?"
- "You have a wonderful talent and I'm sure you'll always enjoy _____ in your spare time, but you must choose something sensible to do for a living."
- "Do you realize how few people actually make it as a/an _____? Your chances of being successful are so small, and I hate for you to set yourself up for disappointment."

Fill in the blanks below with other words of discouragement that have dissuaded you from pursuing your talents as a career or a pastime. If you haven't yet identified what your talent is, think about what may have kept you from doing so.

_____

_____

_____

In the first four chapters of this book, you will be looking at what may have caused you to stop developing the artist within you. You will begin to see that practicing your art is a form of worship, a way to use your talents to draw closer to God. As you look at why you may have been stifled in your artistic development, you will be encouraged to pass quickly through *blame* into *forgiveness.* Still, we will use these first weeks in our artist's daybook (more about that later) to clear out any debris left over from old injuries and begin relinquishing accusation and anger. This act of forgiveness will liberate us from past and future discouragement so that God's creative power can begin to flow through us. Then, in the last four chapters of the book, we will focus on three actions: seeking the inspiration of the Holy Spirit, creating the time, space, and solitude we need to be truly creative, and simplifying our lives to make that time and space more available.

WHAT TO EXPECT

This is the beginning. Before you read more in this book, commit to doing the following either on your own or with a group:

1. To read the weekly chapter and do as many of the exercises as you can.
2. To memorize the scripture verse for each week.
3. To write at least five days a week. The next chapter explains how your artist's daybook can help you begin practicing your art, even if you're not a writer.
4. To pray daily that God will be in charge of the changes that will take place in your life as a result of doing this creative work.
5. If you are in a group, commit to begin and end each group session on time and in prayer. (Come on time if you're going to be on time—and come fifteen minutes early if you're going to be late!)
6. To believe that God gave you your artistic gifts for a reason, that he wants you to use these gifts, and that, no matter how old you are, *it's not too late.*

If you are going through the book as a group, here are a few suggestions of what to do between group meetings. These apply to each chapter in the book. (If you are going through the book on your own, you might keep these guidelines in mind as you read, especially if you are keeping to a one-chapter-a-week schedule.)

- Read the next chapter.
- Memorize the verse at the beginning of the next chapter. Be prepared to recite it at the beginning of next week's meeting.
- Write every morning for twenty minutes in your artist's daybook.
- Complete as many of the exercises in this chapter as you can. They are designed as prompts for journaling, but they can be done separately if you have other things to write about in your daybook. (This will become clearer as you read through chapter 2.)
- Pray for your group members daily. *This cannot be overemphasized.* When you put your life in the Father's hands, when you come together in Jesus' name and seek personal and spiritual growth through the Holy Spirit, God will honor the desires of your heart.

This is the time we begin to recognize God's creative call and to answer it. It's exciting, sometimes even scary work we are doing. Surround yourself with his protection and his grace as you work your way through your artistic awakening. We are God's children. We are here to do his will, not gratify our own egos. Once we understand that, the creative flow we are hoping to generate will begin to course through us.

Do not conform any longer
to the pattern of this world,
but be transformed
by the renewing of your mind.

ROMANS 12:2

CHAPTER TWO

LISTENING

In the morning, O LORD, you hear my voice;
in the morning I lay my requests before you and wait in expectation.

PSALM 5:3

A special silence pervades the house when I first wake up in the morning. I set my alarm to go off before my husband's normal rising time, so I can enjoy this silent time alone. I get up and pour my first cup of coffee for the day, shuffle to my writing desk, light a sandalwood candle, and sit for a moment, listening to the silence and the sounds of the awakening world. This is the time of day when I can best hear what God has to say to me—not in words, but in silence. I pick up my pen and begin to write. I write whatever comes into my mind, sometimes the news of my life, sometimes whatever is troubling me, sometimes a funny story about something that happened the day before. I use my writing time as prayer time, too, thanking God for all his good gifts, asking him for what I need, praying for others, and praising him for the miracle of knowing that he is hearing me and that he will respond.

This time-between-times, this predawn, precious time of listening to God and knowing he is listening to me has become an essential part of my life as an artist. This is the time when my mind has not quite moved from the unconsciousness of sleep into the consciousness of my daytime self. Author Madeleine

L'Engle calls this kind of time "*be*ing time; it's something we all need for our spiritual health, and often we don't take enough of it."[1] *Being time* is the time when we cease to strive. It is about placing ourselves in a state of expectation so that we can hear what God, the Creator, has to say to us, his creation. Being time is the time we ask, "Lord, what would you have me do with the talents you have given me? Guide me in the way that I should go." It is a time when we train ourselves to listen to the silence. L'Engle continues: "As I listen to the silence, I learn that my feelings about art and my feelings about the Creator of the universe are inseparable."[2] Before we can start practicing our art, let's learn to practice the art of listening to what God has to say to us as artists.

LISTENING EXPECTANTLY

Waiting in expectation means waiting to hear what God wants you to hear. The idea of *confidence* is implicit in the word *expectation*. The Greek word for this

EXERCISE 1: HEARING THINGS

Make a list of some of the sounds you hear on an average day, both the pleasant and the unpleasant ones, from the time you get up in the morning until you retire at night.

*Wind, *tires rolling on the trail,
o little girls screaming, *laughter,
*coffee maker gurgling, *music,
o stomping feet, *the engine in my car,
*Doors opening and closing.

Go back and highlight or put a star next to the positive ones and put a zero next to the ones that really annoy you.

concept, the word used in the Septuagint and the New Testament, is *elpizo,* which means "confident expectation," now sometimes translated as the less forceful word *hope.* When David wrote Psalm 5, he knew without question that God would hear him and respond. David did not merely hope. He waited in confident expectation that God would hear him and speak to him. We live in a noisy world. Like David, we need to follow the Lord's admonition to "Be still, and know that I am God" (Psalm 46:10).

As we learn to be still, to cease striving, and to become more aware of all that is going on around us and within us, we will be readying ourselves to be more receptive to hearing God's message to us as artists.

THE ARTIST'S DAYBOOK

In this chapter we'll look at a technique that will force you to give yourself quiet time, to be still so that you will be able to hear what God has to say to you. Like muscles that need to be exercised or a musical instrument that must be practiced, the artist's attitude has to be rehearsed and exercised daily if we want it to develop. To be receptive to God's guidance in nurturing the artist within us, we have to clear the airwaves of the noise and static of our daily lives. We must open a designated line between God and us. The surest way I know to do this is to faithfully—every day if possible—keep a record of our growth as artists. We'll call this record our artist's daybook because we want to start thinking of ourselves as artists. Look at the time you spend in the artist's daybook as part of your journey as an artist. As you develop the habit of spending time alone with God through writing in your daybook, you will understand more clearly the relationship between journaling and listening, between listening and being an artist.

Journaling is not a new idea. Creative thinkers throughout time have regularly set down their thoughts, ideas, and feelings in journals, diaries, or daybooks. The journals of both ordinary and extraordinary people have been the source of much of our recorded history. Many of us can attest to our journals being our companions and our confidantes during the most important times of our lives. Sitting quietly, making time for ourselves alone, pouring out our joy and our sorrow onto the blank pages can be a form of therapy, a gift to ourselves—the gift of simply "*being*."

Keeping a daybook can allow us to chart patterns of behavior that coincide with those especially happy and satisfying times; it can also help us map out passages through those bleak midwinters of life. We can learn to recognize what works and what doesn't work for us by first writing and later reading our daybook entries. Writers may use their daybooks as a source book for ideas, images, characters, dialogue, and plot for other writing. Visual artists often use their journals to jot down ideas for their projects, inspirations that arise from their creative unconscious while they are writing. Musicians can put their poetry to the page in their daybooks and jot down melodies that come to them in the quiet. And every artist can use the daybook to pray to and hear from God.

Several years ago I heard evangelist and writer Peter Lord speak about his book *Hearing God.* He suggested journaling as a way of doing morning devotions and opening ourselves to whatever God may want us to hear each day. Lord keeps his daybook on his computer so that he can access databases and reference Bible passages that come to him during his devotional journaling. He and many others find the speed at which the computer allows them to transfer thoughts onto the page more efficient and less bothersome than writing by hand in a blank book. I like to use a blank book because I can take it with me and write in it when I'm stuck in traffic, early to an appointment, waiting for a show to begin, or stopping somewhere to take time to just *be.* Do whatever works best for you.

I use my daybook as much for praying and trying to hear what God has to say to me as for recording my daily activities and thoughts. Over time my entries have started changing their focus from writing about my life and myself to recognizing and enumerating the ways God shows me that he is in control of my life. Not only have I become more aware of his blessings by focusing on him instead of me, but more blessings seem to come as a result of my giving more attention to God.

God *wants* us to pay attention to him and to ask for what we need. He's just waiting for a chance to show us what an awesome and loving God he is. Writing in our daybooks can be a way of opening up to him, of quieting our overactive minds so we can hear him. It can help us develop the habit of tapping into the creative side of our minds, the part of our brains we don't often use in our daily lives. And it can be a way of recording the personal changes that result from our spending more time waiting to hear what God has to tell us.

"In the Morning, O LORD, You Hear My Voice"

However you use your artist's daybook, you should at least experiment with writing when you first get up each morning. Some creativity experts suggest that keeping a journal unlocks the right side of the brain, the so-called creative side, regardless of the time of day one chooses to write. But I believe writing in the morning has several advantages. Most of us are more vulnerable and in a somewhat more ethereal, dreamlike state first thing in the morning. The world hasn't quite pulled us in yet, and we haven't begun to start putting on the persona we will wear the rest of the day. We're more "real" in the first hour of waking up. What we write can be the most revelatory because we don't have our guard up yet. Journaling in the morning, even if you aren't a "morning person," is one of the most powerful techniques you can use to get back in touch with your creative self. If you do nothing more than start writing every morning for twenty minutes, you will be well on your way to getting in touch with your artist self through the power of the Holy Spirit.

In her provocative little book *Becoming a Writer,* Dorothea Brande contends that those of us who want to be artists have to retrain ourselves to automatically draw upon the unconscious, creative mind, the part of our mind that was predominant when we were children. The first step in becoming an artist, Brande writes, is to regularly practice bringing the unconscious mind to the conscious level so that we can think and live more creatively every day, all day long. One way to do this is to write in your artist's daybook first thing in the morning. "If you are to have the full benefit of the richness of the unconscious you must learn to write [create] easily and smoothly when the unconscious is in the ascendant. *The best way to do this is to rise half an hour, or a full hour, earlier than you customarily rise. Just as soon as you can—and without talking, without reading the morning's paper, without picking up the book you laid aside the night before—begin to write.*"[3] This advice holds an important key for artists of all media and disciplines. When we adopt the habit of writing first thing in the morning, we tap into that deep unconscious source of our creativity. The more regularly we practice this early morning writing, the more we make tapping into the creative reservoir a habit.

What about those of you who prefer to journal at night before you go to bed? I believe that it is certainly better to write in your daybook at night (is it a "nightbook" then?) or in the middle of the day on your lunch break than not to write at all. If you work nights, "morning" may not have the same meaning to you as it does to those who are on a "regular" schedule. My friend Phyllis, a visual artist for whom regular journaling is a newfound and potent practice, says that her best time to write is after the family leaves the house for the day rather than when she first arises in the morning. Another friend, Jackie, finds closure in writing in the evening after all the bustle of the day is behind her. Noted creativity expert Mihaly Csikszentmihalyi has this to say about journaling in general and about journaling at the end of the day in particular: "Most creative people keep a diary, or notes, or lab records to make their experiences more concrete and enduring. If you don't do so already, it might help to start with a very specific task: to record each evening the most *surprising* event that happened that day and your most surprising action."[4] Besides helping you develop the habit of paying attention to the novelty and wonder all around us that most of us never notice,

Csikszentmihalyi contends, writing down our experiences and insights is the best way to keep hold of creative ideas when they come our way.

I wholeheartedly encourage you to write whenever it is best for you, but I strongly suggest that you experiment with early morning writing. This may mean, as Dorothea Brande suggests, getting up half an hour earlier than you usually do (which may mean retiring half an hour earlier each night). But even if the experiment lasts only a week, try writing in the morning and see if what you put on paper isn't of a different quality from what you write in the middle or at the end of your day. You should write every day, or as close to every day as you can, and that may mean writing whenever you can find the time, but you should not discard the idea of meeting God in the morning in your daybook until you've at least given it a try.

Recording the Journey

It is no accident that the words *journal* and *journey* come from the same French root meaning "daily." Your journey through life is your daily walk, and to journal means to keep a daily record of that walk. The artist's daybook, your journal, has several purposes:

- You begin your day focusing on the Creator and start seeing yourself as a partner in his creativity. As you overcome the obstacles that keep you from realizing what God wants you to do with your artistic gifts, you will start to think of yourself as an artist. Writing in your daybook will allow you to record this journey as you become a healthier, holier, and more complete vessel of the Holy Spirit.
- You allow some private time to *kvetch* about all the things that are troubling you. You are allowed to be angry, hurt, afraid, resentful, and even judgmental here. This is a place for you to lay out all that nasty human stuff so both God and you can take a look at it. The first few

weeks may be a time of filling up your artist's daybook with all the garbage you need to offload before you can start to understand God's will for you as an artist. That's okay. You'll get past it.

- You develop the habit of taking time alone. This humble beginning— spending twenty minutes with your artist's daybook each morning—will help you realize that you can make time for the things that are important to you. I try to get up thirty minutes before anyone else in my house in order to have my daybook writing time. My family understands that I'm serious about not wanting to be interrupted the first half-hour of the morning, so even if they are awake, they respect my alone time. If you live with others, try to communicate to them the importance of honoring your time alone.

- You can use your artist's daybook to complete some of the exercises in each chapter of this book. This is a great way to get twice the payoff for your time.

Daybook Guidelines

You don't have to be a writer to keep an artist's daybook. Anyone can follow these basic suggestions for journaling.

Write every day. Or try to write every day, but don't berate yourself on the days it just doesn't happen. You will have a new chance tomorrow. If you miss a day, don't do two entries the next day. Don't worry about catching up. Simply move on.

Just write. Write for twenty minutes without stopping. If you get stuck, keep writing: "I'm stuck. I don't have a thing to say. I've run out of ideas. This would be a good time to pray: 'Our Father who art in heaven.'" Better yet, make up your own prayer. The operative phrase here is *just write.* You'll be amazed at the thoughts and ideas that eventually surface once you get in the habit of writing for twenty minutes every morning.

Write for you and you alone. God is the only one who will ever see this unless you choose to share it, but I recommend that you don't. If you write something wonderful, you can always turn it into a separate piece and share that, but I urge you to protect and respect the privacy of your daybook. It is important that you have a sense of safety that can only come from promising yourself that what you're writing will never be seen by another human being. You are writing to God so that he will help you recognize your authentic artist self. This is a private matter between you and him.

Write as though your creative life depends upon it. It does.

Listening to the Spirit

One thing that makes the artist's daybook so powerful is that it gives us permission to hear what our hearts are saying. We have to learn to quiet the voices, both internal and external, that bombard us daily so that we can hear the voice of the Spirit, who speaks to us through our hearts. This is very difficult for most of us.

> *We do not write in order to be understood, we write in order to understand.*
>
> —C. DAY-LEWIS

Yoga masters spend a lifetime learning to quiet their thoughts, and Christians who want to quiet the noise in their minds in order to hear God often practice *centering prayer,* a form of Christian meditation that dates back to early monastic practices. In centering prayer, individuals spend a certain amount of time each day meditating on a holy word like *Jesus, grace,* or *Spirit* in order to clear their minds of the clutter that normally keeps them from being aware of the promptings of the Holy Spirit. For most of us, the greatest problem is simply stopping the constant flow of words that runs through our minds. To make matters worse, the flow of ideas is much more constant and insistent in creative, divergent thinkers. Artists, especially writers, often just have "too many words."

The artist's daybook is a place to put all those words. As we develop the habit of daily writing and it becomes as much a part of our morning ritual as our first cup of coffee or our shower before dressing, we will find ourselves using our words to get in touch with the Holy Spirit and learn to hear his creative call.

Many writers, composers, and visual artists report that when they are at their creative best, it seems as if something outside themselves takes over. This perception that art is an expression of something moving *through* us rather than *from* us is not limited to Christian artists, but Christians are likely to identify the feeling as the Holy Spirit manifesting himself through them. As you write in your daybook, pray that God will reveal himself to you through the words you write. You will discover that God can use your own words to say what he wants you to hear and what he wants you to express through your art.

WORD PLAY

Writing in your artist's daybook every morning is one way to listen to what God has to tell you. Scripture is another way God speaks to us, and memorizing key passages from Scripture can help open the channels of communication between God and us. The verses at the beginning of each chapter were selected because of what they reveal about our relationship to God as his artists, "called according to his purposes." One of the things I ask you to try as you work through the rest of this book is to memorize the passage at the beginning of each chapter. If you do, the verses will stay with you even after you finish the book. You will notice that different verses come back to you at different times as you practice listening to your world and to your God.

Let's take a few minutes to talk about memory work or, as I prefer to call it, *word play*. Memorizing is a skill many of us have either never developed or haven't used in years. It harks back to elementary school programs, class plays, or lines of Shakespeare we were required to recite in high-school English class. If it has been a long time since you've memorized anything, review the following techniques professional speakers and actors use to learn their lines by heart.

Memory Tips

- First, read carefully and decide what the passage *means*. Something meaningful is much more memorable than a string of words. If you understand the intention of the writer, the words will be easier for you to remember.
- Break down the passage into *short phrases* that seem to go together.
- Memorize an *easy segment* first. Then add harder ones that come before and after it.
- *Daisy-chain* your memory work. First learn one segment. When you know that one, memorize a second and add it to the first. Then add the third to the first and second, and so forth.
- If you are going through *The Creative Call* with a group, memorize your verse over a period of days, not at one sitting or right before your group meeting.
- Find the *rhythm* of the passage and memorize it with a beat, like a nursery rhyme, a rap, or a poem.
- Choose a *keyword* for each phrase and use it as an anchor in case you draw a blank.
- Set the words to a *familiar tune* or make up one of your own.
- Look for *mnemonic devices* like the repetition of certain sounds, how a list of key words might lend itself to an acronym, or the way some words might appear in alphabetical order.
- Use your favorite memorizing technique—and write it down here. (If you are in a group, share what works best for you at your next meeting.)

_____

_____

Developing the right attitude about memorizing these weekly Bible verses is imperative if you want to be successful at it. Work on your passage every day, using your daybook to practice writing it from memory. Recite it while you're exercising or commuting to work, use whatever memorizing strategy works best for you, and you will be "off book" before the end of the week. Practicing and reciting the verse throughout the week will be a blessing on you and the work you're doing to develop the artist within. Don't look at it as memory work; think of it as word play. And this word play might be one of the things you do each morning to prepare yourself for hearing what God has to say to you as an artist.

LISTENING TO OUR PAST

You may not be able to say you were a talented musician, visual artist, or performer when you were young, but if you have read this far, you probably believe that at some point in your life, you were more creative than you are now and you'd like to get that side of yourself back. As you hear God's creative call in your life, it can be helpful to listen to your past. Try to remember a time when you felt more artistic or creative and identify what caused you to quit exercising your talents. In order for the artist within us to be resurrected, we need to recognize the key events that may have led to our burying that part of ourselves in the first place. In chapter 4, we will be dealing with unresolved feelings about people who may have discouraged our artistic development. Right now try to remember the significant *events* that led you away from practicing your art.

Perhaps something traumatic occurred in your life that caused you to give up on being an artist. Or maybe you gradually spent less and less time practicing your art until you were out of the habit of being an artist altogether. Which one of these possibilities is most true for you? (Write it on the line below.)

Spent less and less time.

When I was in high school, I would not only practice piano for the required thirty to sixty minutes a day, but after dinner in the evening, I would sit down at the piano again and play what I wanted to play just for the emotional release. In a similar vein, I recall writing some beautiful essays and poems while listening to Handel's *Water Music* or Dvorak's Symphony no. 5, *The New World,* two pieces of music that stimulated the release of creative energy in me. How could I have ever given up playing the piano and writing, these two forms of self-expression that gave me so much pleasure? For one thing, they took time and energy. I grew up and got busy with other things.

As we grow up and enter our adult lives, we "put off childish things." Unfortunately, the things we put off are often the things that are the most important part of who we are as individuals. If you spend less time doing your art now than you used to, you may want to investigate why.

EXERCISE 2: THE WAY WE WERE

Think back to the last time you felt really creative. How old were you? What were you working on and how did you feel about being an artist at that time?

When we did Calligraphy with Jeanette

You may want to write about this in your daybook or express your thoughts and feelings in some other way. (You might choose to respond to this and any of the exercises in the book with a sketch, a painting, a tapestry, a piece of stained glass, a poem, or a song. Use your particular gift to work through as many of the exercises in each chapter as you can.)

Many people recall a distinct event that triggered a sudden cessation of their artistic effort. For some of us, graduating from high school and going off to college was the point at which we stopped being in the chorus, band, or orchestra, so we gave up singing or playing the flute or violin. Perhaps the turning point for you was getting your first real job and trying to fit into your life all the things that seemed more important than acting in community theater or continuing to draw or paint. Did getting married change your focus to activities that didn't allow for the seclusion most artists require? Did having children? Getting caught up in adult responsibilities? Or maybe you decided at some point that you weren't good enough to ever get anywhere with your talent, so you made the conscious decision to let it go.

EXERCISE 3: "BUT WHY WAIT?"

Finish each of these statements.

I would be practicing my art if only…

had the resources: but why wait?

I'll start making time for my art when…

I feel like it :) : but why wait?

I'd be doing my art now if it weren't for…

money being an issue: but why wait?

Now go back and add this to the end of each of your three statements: *But why wait?* You have just turned these negative messages into statements of hope.

The important thing is that creation is God's, and that we are part of it, and being part of creation is for us to be co-creators with [him] in the continuing joy of new creation.

—MADELEINE L'ENGLE

Proverbs 13:12 teaches us that "Hope deferred makes the heart sick, but a longing fulfilled is a tree of life." God wants us to act with hopeful hearts, not to continually put off working toward our heart's desires, not to postpone our artistic development and feel frustrated and empty as a result. As you do the work of seeking God's vision and reviving your talents, consider now what you have hoped for and longed for.

EXERCISE 4: HOPES AND LONGINGS

Complete each of these statements.

I always hoped that I'd…

being able to supply for or with my family.

I wish I had the courage to…

help others excel

If I could go back in time, I would…

not be a jerk to my best friend

Write in your daybook for ten minutes about a "hope deferred." Tell why it was deferred, how your life would be different if it had not been deferred, and how you might be able to actualize that hope today.

By listening to our past, paying attention to the voice of hope that resides deep within us, and overcoming our fear of pursuing those "hopes deferred," we will peel away the layers of self-protection that keep us from hearing what God wants to tell us about the artist he has created us to be.

MERGING AND PURGING

The second or third time I taught the material in what is now *The Creative Call,* I received an e-mail message from a group member who was having trouble getting motivated to keep his artist's daybook in the morning. I wrote him back, encouraging him to think of it not as another chore or burden, but as an opportunity. "Journaling…the daybook…whatever you want to call it…is all about emptying yourself. This is where all the stuff in the dark corners can come out into the light of day. Getting in touch with what is bothering you, what you are anxious about, what you fear, how you feel—good or bad—and getting it out there on the page frees you up from processing it the rest of the day. That's why it's so healthy to write in the morning. And the added blessing for Christians is that we tell the Father all our concerns. As we lay those burdens down at his feet, our words naturally go to prayer. By the time we've finished our fifteen to twenty minutes of writing, we have 'merged and purged': merged with God and purged ourselves of the anxieties that might have plagued us all day long if we hadn't taken this time to unload. Does that make sense?"

I should have added that once one acquires the habit of keeping a daybook, especially in the morning, it actually becomes something a person looks forward to, something that's *fun.*

Think of your artist's daybook as starting your day with an offering to God. Believe that in the morning he hears your voice. Then "wait in expectation" and in the assurance that God will communicate with you through "the words of [your] mouth and the meditation of [your] heart" (Psalm 19:14).

Learning to hear God's voice despite the cacophony of our everyday lives is something that will take time. Reading his Word, memorizing passages that speak to our desire to reawaken the artist within us, and writing regularly in our artist's daybook are ways of quieting our minds so that we can hear God's voice as we offer our words to him. We end chapter 2 with an exercise that reminds us of how potent, powerful, and fun our words can be.

EXERCISE 5: FAVORITE WORDS

For the next ten minutes, list all your favorite words. They do not have to be in any particular order. (You may want to start your list here then continue it in your daybook.)

Start with something easy like adjectives: *soft, mauve, juicy, lovely, sensuous, sinuous.* When you think of your first noun, switch to nouns. If you write *rainbow,* think of favorite color words. If you write *forest,* think of all the forest-related words that you love. People, places, smells, foods, natural objects, textures, phrases from songs, emotions—you have no restrictions.

Simply write for ten minutes. Refer back to this list from time to time and add to it whenever you can.

love	faith	trust
hope	refresh	thrive
breathe	nourish	spices
tart	coconut	concoction
epiphany		

In *Writing for Your Life,* Deena Metzger discusses the practice and the difficulty of journaling: "Sometimes the first minutes of writing are simply a process of priming the pump. The act of sitting still with the blank page or of writing as a leap of faith is an offering, a gesture of sincerity that one makes to the creative unconscious. Not always, but sometimes, after much discouragement, the writing gushes forth like a geyser from the center of the earth."[5] If we practice the discipline of daily writing, of offering to God a "gesture of sincerity" in faith that he desires us to use the gifts he has given us, we will find that God is speaking to us through his Holy Spirit and that we can learn to hear him.

May the words of my mouth
and the meditation of my heart
be pleasing in your sight,
O LORD, my Rock and my Redeemer.

PSALM 19:14

CHAPTER THREE

AWAKENING

All who are skilled among you are to come
and make everything the LORD has commanded.

EXODUS 35:10

As I write this chapter, I am listening to a CD by guitarist Christopher Parkening called *Simple Gifts*. In the late 1970s Parkening had achieved such fame and financial security as a classical musician that he was able to realize his lifelong dream: to retire at the age of thirty, move to a ranch in Montana, and spend his time fly-fishing. His talent and hard work as a recording and concert artist had paid off, and at an age where most of us are just figuring out what we want to be when we grow up, Parkening discontinued recording contracts and concert tours and retired from his musical career. A real success story, right? Well, yes, but not in the way you might think.

What followed for Parkening was a realization that, although he had realized all his dreams, he wasn't happy. Something was missing. He had used his great talent, reached the apex of his career, and then retired from the art world only to discover that, as the writer of Ecclesiastes bemoans, "Meaningless! Meaningless!... Everything is meaningless!"

After about four years, Parkening had an awakening. He was visiting friends in California, and a neighbor invited him to attend Grace Community Church. Parkening describes his experience:

> John MacArthur preached a sermon which he titled, "Examine your-
> selves, whether you be in the faith," from Matthew 7, where Jesus
> said, "Not everyone that saith unto me, 'Lord, Lord' shall enter into
> the kingdom of heaven; but he that does the will of my Father which
> is in heaven…" When he spoke those words from the Bible, my
> whole life flashed in front of me. I thought, "I'm not a Christian!" I
> would stand before Christ, and He would say to me, "You never cared
> about the things of Christ. You never cared about being obedient to
> my commands. You never cared about glorifying me with your life or
> your music…"
>
> That night I went home, broken over my sins and the emptiness
> of my life, the wasted opportunities with the guitar, and playing the
> instrument for the wrong motives. I asked Christ to come into my
> life. And I remember saying, "Whatever you want me to do, Lord,
> I'll do it."

Inspired by 1 Corinthians 10:31, "Whatever you do, do it all for the glory of God," in 1982 Parkening decided to come out of retirement with the CD *Simple Gifts*. This collection of fourteen sacred songs and anthems, including several by J. S. Bach, is Christopher Parkening's "phoenix song," his rising again from the ashes of his early retirement. He says:

> I had always been inspired, even growing up, by the music of Bach.
> But even more so when I read what he said about music: "The aim
> and final reason of all music is none else but the glory of God."

Parkening discovered that Bach regularly inscribed the beginning of his scores with the letters *J. J.,* which stood for the Latin "Jesu, Juva," or "Jesus, help." At the end of a composition, he often wrote *S.D.G.* for "Soli Deo Gloria," or "To God alone the glory." Parkening continues:

> I thought if Bach could use his great ability and talent for that purpose, that would be the least that I could do with whatever ability or talent God had given me.... I realize honestly that whatever talent or ability any of us has been given, it has been given to us by God, and we're responsible to be good stewards of that talent.[1]

SIMPLE GIFTS

Does this story inspire you to start using your talents, to awaken or reawaken "whatever ability or talent God had given [you]"? Many music critics describe Christopher Parkening as the finest classical guitarist since André Segovia. "Sure," we might say, "if someone has that kind of remarkable gift, then he or she *does* have the responsibility to share it with the world and to use it for the glory of God. But my ability is so...well, average. God doesn't expect me to become a world famous writer, artist, or musician. How dare I compare myself with the giants in my field?" The fear of not being "good enough" can keep us from using our talents and gifts, especially if those gifts have lain dormant for quite a while.

The problem with this kind of thinking, apart from the fact that it's self-defeating, is that it is based on assumptions that we have no right to make. To begin with, it is not our place to decide for ourselves whether we are "good enough" to glorify God with our talent. This is ironic because denigrating ourselves *feels* like humility. How can our meager gifts and talents be used by God? How dare we believe we will ever be good enough to express ourselves openly, let alone good enough to make a living using our talents? How conceited are we to think our gifts can actually touch the lives of others? This self-effacing attitude seems anything but arrogant, yet arrogant is exactly what it is. By adopting this attitude, we assume that we know best what to do with our gifts: to bury them and avoid public humiliation.

Secondly, comparing ourselves to others is pointless because we don't know how God intends to use us once we let him have his way with us. Do we really think God would give us a talent and then provide no venue for it? You don't have to become world renowned to influence other people through your art.

So ask yourself, "How dare I question God's plans for me in his world? Who am I to presume to know what God can or cannot do with my talents?"

EXERCISE 1: VISIONS AND LONGINGS

What were your favorite things to do when you were a child? Mentally put yourself into different venues—for example, with your family, with your friends, at school, at Girl Scouts or Boy Scouts, with your church group, indoors, outside. Try to remember the activities you really loved and looked forward to doing. List as many of these as you can in the next five minutes. (Use your daybook if you need more space.)

_____

_____

_____

_____

_____

_____

_____

The list of favorite pastimes you just wrote probably includes many hands-on creative activities that are simple, free, or low-cost and limited only by time and imagination: building a snow fort or a sand castle, finger painting, blowing bubbles, making clover necklaces, picking a bouquet of wild flowers and taking them home for your mother, baking cookies, riding your bike, sitting by a lake. Think of all the simple yet delightful things you did as a child that brought you joy and satisfaction.

Exercise 1 helps us realize that all of us were given the gift of creativity. Some are more artistically talented in certain areas than others, but even if our talent is as seemingly mundane as keeping a beautiful yard or a lovely home, we all have simple gifts we can choose to either develop or bury. How can God use *your* "simple gifts," even if they seem only average to you? One answer to that lies in the diversity of people he has created. Let me explain.

The world is comprised of billions of individuals, and each person responds emotionally and intellectually to art. But what might move one person to tears will only elicit a yawn from someone else. Louis Comfort Tiffany, for instance, endured throughout his life a wide range of vacillation in public opinion of his work. Founder of the Art Nouveau movement in the United States and considered a master artist in the design of glass, jewelry, and pottery, Tiffany saw his work viewed with contempt by both artists and critics of the modernist movement. Yet less than one hundred years later, his lamps sell at auction for hundreds of thousands of dollars.

Similarly, someone who is deeply moved by the writings of C. S. Lewis might not appreciate the ubiquitous *Chicken Soup* books. Yet how many people have been stirred by the stories in those books? And consider the art of Thomas Kinkade, who has sold millions of prints, paintings, gift articles, and books: His work is pabulum to many art aficionados. Yet God has used Kinkade, "the painter of light," to touch the hearts of many people who long for a simpler, gentler world.

It is not for us to question how God will use our gifts. It is instead our responsibility to realize that God gave our talents to us for a purpose, *his* purpose, and it's not important that we understand what that purpose is before we start becoming productive artists. What is important is that we accept the talents God gave us, develop them, honor them, use them, and not bury them.

 ...God Who, in His mercy, completes the hidden and mysterious work of creation in us by enlightening our minds and hearts, by awakening in us the awareness that we are words spoken in His One Word and that Creating Spirit (Creator Spiritus) [which] dwells in us, and we in him.

—THOMAS MERTON

Many people are familiar with the parable, found in Matthew 25:14-30, about the three servants who were given "talents" by their master to take care of while he was gone on a long journey. Two of the servants put the talents out at interest and returned to their master double his original investment. The third servant, out of fear, buried his talent and gave back to his master the original amount, unimproved and undeveloped. The master was so angry with him that he took away the one talent the servant had been given and instructed his steward to "throw that worthless servant outside, into the darkness, where there will be weeping and gnashing of teeth" (25:30). The two servants who had done something productive with their talents were praised and rewarded: "His master replied, 'Well done, good and faithful servant! You have been faithful with a few things; I will put you in charge of many things. Come and share your master's happiness!'" (25:23). I believe Jesus told this parable to admonish all of us, whether talented in the arts or in other aspects of life, to use and develop the talents we have been given. Like Christopher Parkening, we need to realize that being "successful" is not synonymous with having fame and financial security and early retirement. Being successful is synonymous with doing God's will. The story of the servant who buried the talents his master had given him has greater meaning when put alongside this contemporary parable of Christopher Parkening choosing to use, rather than bury, his gift. Keep these stories in mind as you work through the rest of your exercises for this week.

EXERCISE 2: CALLED BY NAME

The scripture verse at the beginning of this chapter, Exodus 35:10, was spoken to the craftsmen and artisans commissioned to build the tabernacle and the Ark of the Covenant. The spirit of the words, a calling for "all who are skilled" to come and make everything the Lord has commanded, can apply to your painting, music, writing, drawing, acting, dancing, needlework, landscaping, or composing.

Read Exodus 35:30-35, taking note of the fact that the main artists who worked on the Ark of the Covenant and the tabernacle were actually *called by name* in the Bible. What do you think it means that the Bible includes not only the names of great kings, warriors, and prophets, but also the names of artists who worked on the place where the very Word of God, the Ten Commandments, was to be kept?

_____

_____

_____

_____

In your daybook, write about your talent or talents and how you have both used and buried them throughout your life. What key events or periods of your life influenced how you either developed or hid your talent?

"BAND KIDS"

Contemporary society and its values are at least partly responsible for people's choosing to hide or ignore their talents. I've been teaching students designated as *gifted* for many years, and I have noticed that when young children are accepted into gifted programs, parents, almost without exception, are overjoyed by the news that they have an exceptional child. The kids are excited to know that they will be going to a special class with other "smart kids." They have to be cautioned, however, not to make too big a deal about being in the program, or the other kids will see them as bragging (and insufferable). But no matter how humble they try to be about it, envy on the part of the other children, taboos against being singled out as different, and inordinate parental expectations can lead these children to regret their gifted designation by the time they get to middle school and high school. As early as fifth or sixth grade, they begin to disguise their exceptionality in order to fit in with their peers. As these children grow older, more and more of them drop out of gifted classes in favor of the more mainstream honors classes, which are aimed at high achievers but not highly creative, divergent thinkers.

Research on gifted and talented children has shown that musically or artistically gifted children are likely to be labeled "dweebs" or "nerds" by their contemporaries and even by some of their teachers. Anyone who was a band kid in school knows what I am talking about. The band at my high school consisted of some of the most intelligent, talented, witty, and interesting people on campus. With few exceptions, however, these students were not among the "popular" kids. How many young people, because of the negative social stigma attached to these pursuits, have given up music or theater before they had a chance to see how good they could be—and how fulfilling it is to develop their talents? It is still true today that walking around with a violin case is not as cool as walking around with a cheerleader's pom-pom.

Yet I'd like a dollar for every time I hear an adult say, "I sure wish my parents hadn't given in when I wanted to quit the band (or piano lessons, or dancing lessons, or art lessons)." Does this sound familiar to you? If so, you need to write down the following sentence and keep it where you will see it every day:

IT IS NEVER TOO LATE TO RESURRECT MY GIFTS AND TALENTS, SO WHY WAIT?

As we awaken our talents, we might do well to follow Solomon's advice in Proverbs 3:5: "Trust in the LORD with all your heart and lean not on your own understanding." Our own understanding is likely to generate a long list of reasons for not doing our art. Trusting in the Lord is the key to moving past all the "buts" that keep us from acting on the desires of our hearts. Those desires are from God. *Believe it.* This next exercise is designed to get you in touch with those places where you are not fully trusting in God's provision for you as an artist, his provision of time, money, or something else.

EXERCISE 3: TRUST IN THE LORD

Fill in the blanks with whatever comes to mind. Elaborate on one of your responses when you write in your artist's daybook one day this week.

If I could trust in the Lord's provision, I would…

_____

_____

If I could trust in the Lord's provision, I would…

_____

_____

If I could trust in the Lord's provision, I would…

_____

_____

Maybe you feel as though trust is not the issue. Perhaps you clearly understand that God is the one from whom all blessings flow, and you believe he is a faithful provider. So what else is keeping you from developing your artistic abilities? The next exercise will help you determine what you specifically need in order to begin.

EXERCISE 4: WHAT I NEED

Make a list of *what you need* to begin practicing your art. What do you really need? Time? A place to paint? Supplies? A new flute? Money for a refresher course? The courage to join a writers' group? Voice lessons?

List your needs below.

_____

_____

_____

_____

_____

_____

_____

_____

_____

Give the Lord an opportunity to demonstrate his interest in you and his power to help you realize your dreams: Ask God for what you need and see what you will receive. In your daybook, write a prayer asking for the ability to see his plan for your artist self and your life. Pray your prayer daily.

One Small Step

Christopher Parkening may not have come out of retirement by starting to keep a daybook, by setting up a workspace for practicing, or by getting his family to support him in his desire to start giving his talent back to the world. He was a well-known musician, so his first step might have been to call his recording studio or his agent and announce that he was ready to start working again. *Our* first step may be a much smaller one, but in some ways much more difficult. Once we take that step, however, the journey gets easier.

> *When God sends His inspiration, it comes to us with such miraculous power that we are able to "arise from the dead" and do the impossible. The remarkable thing about spiritual initiative is that the life and power comes after we "get up and get going." God does not give us overcoming life—He gives us life as we overcome.*
>
> —Oswald Chambers

The year I wrote the first version of this book, I was studying another book on creativity with a group of Christians. The group included a young woman who was struggling to finish her college degree, work part time, and raise two kids on her own. She came to the group faithfully, but even if she had read her chapter for the week, she would rarely have written in her journal. At first she thought lack of time kept her from writing, but later she admitted that something blocked her from getting started. It may have been fear of failure, fear of what she might discover about herself, or fear that there wasn't anything artistic about her after all. It could have been just inertia. The group continued to encourage her to take that first step, to write something—create anything—to get past this stuck place. Her difficulty in getting started seemed to stem from a basic lack of trust in both herself and in God's grace. She just couldn't do it.

You may be feeling this way too. Read what Madeleine L'Engle has to say about overcoming fear and trusting God in *Walking on Water:*

There is much that the artist must trust. He must trust himself. He must trust his work. He must open himself to revelation, and that is an act of trust.… We trust as Lady Julian of Norwich [a medieval Christian writer] trusted, knowing that despite all the pain and horror of the world, ultimately God's loving purpose will be fulfilled and "all shall be well and all shall be well and all manner of thing shall be well." And this all-wellness underlies true art (Christian art) in all disciplines, an all-wellness that does not come to us because we are clever or virtuous, but which is a gift of Grace.[2]

The purpose of the final exercise in this chapter is to help you step out in faith, not because you are good enough or clever enough or virtuous enough, but because God is. If you've been stuck at the starting gate, this exercise might get you off and running. If you're already working at your art, this activity will give you permission to play.

EXERCISE 5: TAKE ONE BABY STEP FORWARD

Draw a picture, write a poem or essay, or shoot a roll of film (or put those great pictures you've already taken into an album). Practice a piece you knew when you were in high school, buy new guitar strings, or call the piano tuner and make an appointment. Buy a new daybook, one art supply, or a new filter for your camera. If money is tight, use what you have. Check out thrift stores and garage sales. The Lord is waiting to see your efforts so he can bless you. Write below how you got past one "If only…I would." Expand on this in your artist's day book.

This week I took the following small step:

_____

_____

Throughout this week and the weeks to come, whether you are writing in your artist's daybook, observing the world around you, praying, listening to the prompting of the Spirit, exercising, or taking care of the ordinary tasks of daily living, remind yourself that you are awakening. Be gentle with yourself, but banish the idea that you can wait until you are "in the mood" or "inspired" to get busy with your art. This journey is not about doing what we *feel* like doing; it's about doing what we *must*. As L'Engle says, "Inspiration far more often comes during the work than before it because the largest part of the job of the artist is to listen to the work and to go where it tells him to go."[3]

> *Commit your work to the LORD,*
> *and your plans will be established.*
> —PROVERBS 16:3, RSV

CHAPTER FOUR

FORGIVING

*Bear with each other and forgive whatever grievances
you may have against one another. Forgive as the Lord forgave you.*

COLOSSIANS 3:13

When Mary was nearing high-school graduation, she told her guidance counselor that she wanted to pursue the desire of her heart—to illustrate children's books. The counselor disdainfully told her, "You can't do that. You've got to be practical. Get a degree in English so you can teach." Ignoring that advice, Mary got a job at an art supply shop, learned all she could about different media and how to use them, and got to know all kinds of working artists. Once she realized that people actually *did* make a living as artists, she turned her energies and talents toward making her dream a reality. Mary Englebreit overcame the discouraging words of others to become one of the world's most successful commercial artists.

Whenever she became disheartened, Englebreit would remember how, even at a young age, her parents had encouraged her to pursue her artwork. When she was nine, Mary announced that she needed a studio, and her mother promptly converted a linen closet into one for her. "From that time on," Englebreit says, "my parents always treated my art as serious business. Bolstered by their support, I continued on even without formal training, telling myself over and over what they had instilled in me: 'Of course you can become an artist. Keep working on it. If you can imagine it, you can achieve it. If you can dream it, you can become it.'"[1]

Englebreit's story illustrates the critical role parents, friends, and spouses play as sources of encouragement for artists. The fact that artistic encouragement is so rare might explain why many of us did not believe that if we dreamed it, we could become it. In this chapter, we'll take a look at the encouragers and discouragers in our lives. We will consider how their attitudes either aided or inhibited our artistic development. Then we'll deal with the issue of forgiveness so that we can free ourselves to become the dreamers and doers God has given us the talent to be.

Ya Gotta Have Heart

Encouragement and *discouragement* both derive from *cor*, Latin for "heart," the same root as the word *courage*. According to the *American Heritage College Dictionary*, *encourage* means "to inspire with hope, courage, or confidence; to give support to, foster." *Discourage* means "to deprive of confidence, hope, or spirit." (We'll be addressing the words *spirit* and *inspiration* in the next chapter.) The encouragers in our lives are those who have helped us *take heart* and find courage to become the people God intends us to be. The discouragers are the ones who disapproved of any designs we had to follow our hearts rather than our heads in choosing our life's pursuit. Discouragers may or may not have intended to cause us to be "fainthearted" and give up on our goals, but regardless of their intentions, the result of their discouragement was the same. Lacking the courage to believe in and follow our dreams, we learned to close our eyes to our visions. Our confidence in our ability to succeed was eroded by discouraging messages coming from the people who knew and loved us most.

My sister Norma earned a degree in fine arts through talent, hard work, determination, scholarships, and student loans. She is an excellent muralist and does beautiful painting on handmade and antique furniture. Her oil paintings grace many elegant homes and businesses in North Carolina where she lives. For years she has been able to make a living working part-time as an artist while remaining a stay-at-home wife and mother. She succeeded despite the lack of encouragement she received from our parents, who simply could not imagine her making a living as an artist. Norma remembers announcing her intention to attend the Columbus School of Art and Design after high school. Our parents responded by telling her that she really didn't have enough talent to be an artist and that she would be wasting her time and money if she went to art school. This is hardly a Mary Englebreit story.

Discouragement like this would have devastated most eighteen-year-olds, but Norma took heart from a mentor outside the family who believed in her and her talent. Her art teacher's support gave Norma the courage to pursue her dream. Now in her mid-forties, Norma has just completed her master's degree in art and is finally producing what she has always wanted to create rather than what other people wanted her to do. She long ago forgave our parents for not being more supportive of her goals when she was young. Now that she has an eighteen-year-old of her own, she understands even more clearly how they were looking out for her best interests as they saw them. After all, how many parents *would* encourage their children to become "starving artists"?

Is there someone in your life whose discouragement may have kept you from realizing your potential as an artist? Did you or do you have to overcome some-one's discouragement in order to become an artist? If you need to forgive anyone for their lack of encouragement at an important turning point in your life, write their names here:

_____

_____

_____

Letting Go

The *American Heritage College Dictionary* defines *forgiveness* as "the act of granting pardon without harboring resentment." It is the willingness to move past the offense and to refuse to entertain further thoughts about it. Forgiveness is not just something we grant another person. It is a gift we give ourselves. It means letting someone off the hook and freeing ourselves from the bad feelings about whatever that person did. After all, a lack of forgiveness hooks us as well as the person who has wronged us. God has instructed us to forgive one another not only in order to maintain harmony among people, but because lack of forgiveness is a trap and a burden to the one who needs to forgive.

In order to understand forgiveness, we first need to recognize that forgiveness is not the same as telling the other person that what they did (or neglected to do) is really okay. It was not okay; it was real, it was negative, and it kept you from having the confidence you needed to pursue your dreams. Whatever their motives, what they did was damaging and wrong. Forgiveness is not giving them your retroactive approval or admitting that maybe you have been too hard on them all these years. Forgiveness is your willingness to truly let go of the negative feelings you may still harbor because of what you feel that person did that hurt you.

 This is the covenant that I will make with them…says the Lord: I will put my laws on their hearts, and write them on their minds…I will remember their sins and their misdeeds no more.

—HEBREWS 10:16-17, RSV

Even the greatest heroes of the Bible needed forgiveness. God's grace to David after David committed adultery with Bathsheba is one of the best illustrations of God's willingness to forgive when we seek him.[2] Colossians 3:13 reminds us, "Bear with each other and forgive whatever grievances you may have against one another. Forgive as the Lord forgave you." The Lord's Prayer addresses our need not only to *receive* forgiveness but to *grant* forgiveness to others.[3] Author Tobias Wolff writes, "The Lord's Prayer…seems to say those things that need to be said every day. It recognizes that we ourselves are not fountains of forgiveness and helps us to be forgiving."[4] Just as God covers our sins with his grace and promises to forget that they ever even existed, we need to cover others' sins by offering them our forgiveness. We also need to believe that God will give us the strength it takes to "commit" this act of forgiveness.

EXERCISE 1: FORGIVING AS GOD FORGIVES US

Choose a person from the list of "discouragers" you made earlier in the chapter:

_____

Write a letter telling the person what he or she did (or neglected to do) that discouraged you in your dream of becoming an artist. Tell the person what you remember, how it made you feel then, and maybe even how it *still* makes you feel. Explain that you are forgiving them to free *yourself* from resentment, not because whatever they did was right or understandable. This exercise is about releasing negative feelings, not condoning unconscionable behavior. Use the lines below to jot down some ideas to put into your letter. Then write your letter in your daybook as one of your entries this week. Even if you never send the letter, this act of forgiveness will free your soul.

_____

_____

_____

_____

Your parents and teachers can't undo what they did or didn't do to help you find your artist voice, but you have the power to change the results of what they did. You can choose, with God's help, to put down that heavy burden of blame and resentment so you can be ready for the indwelling of the Holy Spirit. It is that indwelling, not some message from the past about not being good enough, that will propel you toward becoming the artist God intends for you to be.

So what keeps us from welcoming the cleansing power of forgiveness—not just the forgiveness we receive, but the forgiveness we have the power to grant? It might be habit or stubbornness or a prideful sense of righteous indignation. How can we let "them" off the hook after all the damage they did to us? How can we forgive them when they might not even be willing to admit they ever did anything that requires forgiveness? We want paybacks; we want divine retribution; we want justice.

But justice and forgiveness have nothing to do with one another. Remember, we forgive in order to set our own spirits free, not to condone the misguided actions of someone else. "Most of us who are reluctant to forgive are stuck in our reluctance," write Joanna Laufer and Kenneth S. Lewis. "We really do not want to. When our hardness melts away and we choose to forgive, what had once seemed like compromise and weakness now seems more in line with movement, growth and love."[5] This statement expresses exactly what our attitude toward forgiveness must be: an act of setting ourselves, as well as the one who has offended us, free.

Moving On

We also need to understand that forgiveness is not the same thing as allowing ourselves to be victims of someone's words or misdeeds. We artists can be fragile creatures, especially when it comes to our art, and many of us let the negative comments or discouraging words of others affect us far more than is healthy. Those words only have as much power as we give them, and it is possible to offer forgiveness without allowing our artist selves to continue to be undermined by thoughtless words or advice. We can take those "downers," those deflating comments, and get "uppity" with them. Try the following exercise.

EXERCISE 2: GETTING UPPITY WITH DOWNERS

For each of the discouraging statements below, write some back talk that refutes it.

Example:

(Downer) "You should be doing something worthwhile with
    your time."
(Uppity comeback) "If my art enriches someone else's life—
    or my own—then it is worthwhile."

(Downer) "Nobody will take your art seriously."
(Uppity comeback)

_____

_____

(Downer) "You'll never make a living at your art."
(Uppity comeback)

_____

_____

(Downer) "You don't have enough talent to be a(n) _____ ."
(Uppity comeback)

_____

_____

Part of becoming mature adults is realizing that we will probably never receive the complete support and approval we crave from our parents and other significant people in our lives. All we can do is learn to take in the encouragement that they are able and willing to offer. Then, if we can rise above the well-meaning discouragement they sometimes seem all *too* willing and able to give, we can take heart and press forward with confidence.

ENCOURAGING VOICES

My mother and I were having coffee in an outdoor cafe in Brighton, England, after touring the indescribably opulent Royal Pavilion. I was in my forties then, and I had just explained to my mother how different my reaction to the beauty of the palace was compared to what it would have been when I was in my twenties. A woman at the table next to us said, "Pardon me for eavesdropping, but I overheard what you just said, and I liked how you said it so well that I've written it down. Do you mind if I repeat it to you so that I can see if I got it right?" What an encouragement her words were for the writer in me! How delightful to realize that my words could impress someone to the extent that she would want to write them down exactly as I had spoken them.

It turned out that Caroline, the woman who spoke to me, was also in her late forties and understood exactly what I meant. For the next half-hour, we discussed how our priorities and our focus change as we grow older. Caroline's request that I repeat my words was a turning point in my confidence to pursue writing as a vocation. Encouragement often comes when we least expect it.

When we were children, we found our encouragement in the words and actions of adults. In fact, children in general view themselves largely through the eyes and responses of primary caregivers. But as we grow older, our encourage-

ment comes from other sources: from friends and teachers, from complete stran-
gers—like Caroline in Brighton—who validate that we have something worthwhile to express, and from our heavenly Father himself.

As we saw in the preceding chapter, we as artists are among God's special
people. In Exodus, God honors some important artists by actually calling them
by name:

> Then Moses said to the Israelites, "See, the LORD has chosen Bezalel
> son of Uri, the son of Hur, of the tribe of Judah, and he has filled him
> with the Spirit of God, with skill, ability and knowledge in all kinds
> of crafts—to make artistic designs for work in gold, silver and bronze,
> to cut and set stones, to work in wood and to engage in all kinds of
> artistic craftsmanship. And he has given both him and Oholiab son of
> Ahisamach, of the tribe of Dan, the ability to teach others. He has
> filled them with skill to do all kinds of work as craftsmen, designers,
> embroiderers in blue, purple and scarlet yarn and fine linen, and
> weavers—all of them master craftsmen and designers." (Exodus
> 35:30-35)

During the Babylonian captivity, as the Bible specifically states, the "craftsmen and artists," along with the Jewish king and other important officials,
were carried off to Babylon. In Jeremiah 24:1 we read, "Jehoiachin son of
Jehoiakim king of Judah and the officials, the craftsmen and the artisans of Judah
were carried into exile from Jerusalem to Babylon by Nebuchadnezzar king of
Babylon."

First Chronicles 25:1 tells us, "David, together with the commanders of the
army, set apart some of the sons of Asaph, Heman and Jeduthun for the ministry
of prophesying, accompanied by harps, lyres and cymbals." The writers of
1 Chronicles then list, again by name, all those who were "set apart" to provide

music for the temple services. In those days prophesying had more to do with singing God's praises and edifying God through worship than it did with telling the future, so often the prophets and the musicians were one and the same. God used music to inspire and bring his people closer to him. "All these men were under the supervision of their fathers for the music of the temple of the LORD, with cymbals, lyres and harps, for the ministry at the house of God.... All of them [were] trained and skilled in music for the LORD—they numbered 288" (25:6-7).

If the Lord honored craftsmen, artists, and musicians throughout the history of his chosen people, then surely he treasures the artists and craftsmen of today. Why should we harbor resentment or anger against someone who discouraged us when we have a Father who has given us the gift of creativity, who knows us by name, and is always there to *encourage* us? We need to focus on our heavenly Father's encouragement when we feel hurt, angered, or discouraged by others.

And let's not forget the other ways God gives us encouragement. In the acknowledgments at the beginning of this book, I cite my good friend Marilynda who told me year after year when my Christmas letter arrived, "Janice, you need to become a writer. You have a gift, a way with words, and you need to write." She, and others like her, deserves credit for bringing me to where I am today in my writing career. God gives us encouraging voices throughout our life; we need to learn how to hear them.

Spend some time this week thinking about the people who have been your biggest fans, your *encouragers,* those who help you "take heart." These people believe you will accomplish your goals. They help you trust your own ability. But they don't simply praise you for everything you do without any discernment. They are people you can trust to be honest, who will give you the kind of authentic reflective feedback you need to stay grounded yet confident. And don't forget the encouragement you receive by studying the great artists. Whose work helped you decide that you wanted to become an artist "just like them"?

The purpose of the following exercise is to give you a visual reminder of all the people who, directly or indirectly, have encouraged you to develop your talents. We need to be reminded that for every person who has held us back in our desire to develop our artistic side, there are others who have been an example and an inspiration to us. These are our artist heroes.

EXERCISE 3: MY HEROES

In your daybook, brainstorm a list of all the people who have in any way inspired or encouraged you to believe in yourself as an artist.

Think about all the Marilyndas in your life, those people who kept saying, "You should be a writer…" or "You should paint more—you really have a talent…" or "You should cut a CD—these songs and the way you perform them are wonderful."

Then think about the artists, musicians, writers, performers, and craftsmen whose stories or whose work encourages you. These artists can be people you actually know or famous people you admire. Don't limit yourself to your area of art only. Consider musicians, fine artists, composers, potters, glassworkers, jewelers, sculptors, writers, dancers, actors, directors, and singers. Feel free to include some of the artists I've mentioned in this book.

Now write all these names on a large piece of paper. Use pictures or symbols of the artist tools you associate with each encourager to illustrate your poster. Title and hang it on the wall in your artist workspace.

YOUR OWN WORST ENEMY

Now that you have begun to deal with the ghosts of discouragement past and have looked at the power of encouragement, consider your own attitudes about yourself as an artist and how you might be getting in your own way. We need to look at our own negative attitudes and habits not as something else to feel bad

---

EXERCISE 4: DREAMERS AND DOERS

Respond to each of these questions by writing true or false in the blank.

1. _____ When I was a child, I had a specific dream of what I wanted to become when I grew up. *If this is true for you, what was that dream?*

_____

_____

_____

2. _____ I remember at least one teacher who encouraged me to be more or do more than I believed I could do or be. *If this is true for you, who was that teacher?*

_____

_____

What did that teacher encourage in you?

_____

_____

_____

about, but as something to exorcise from our repertoire of coping mechanisms. We need to forgive ourselves.

I once heard a sermon titled "Living Your Vision" at a church I was visiting. The message made me realize how limited my own vision for my life has been. Why didn't I grow up like Mary Englebreit, who believed that she could achieve whatever goal she set for herself? I now realize that I have been my own worst

---

3. _____ When I was in school, I felt successful in one or more specific areas. *If this is true for you, in what areas were you successful?*

_____

_____

4. _____ I grew up believing that God has a plan for my life; my job was to seek his will for me and make sure my vision was in line with his. *If this is true for you, what is your understanding of God's plan for your life?*

_____

_____

5. _____ To some extent, I pursued my youthful vision into adulthood. *If this is true for you, what aspect of your dream did you follow?*

_____

_____

6. _____ I have recently developed or rekindled a specific vision for my life. *If this is true for you, explain how you are keeping the dream alive.*

_____

_____

enemy because rather than risking failure, I never allowed myself to believe I could accomplish anything extraordinary. Why didn't I set goals the way Englebreit did? Why was fear so much more powerful in me than my desire to become a writer? When did I stop believing that "If I can dream it, I can do it"?

This exercise can tell you some important things about yourself. If you responded "true" to most of these statements, then you are a person who, at some time in your life, has had a life vision and believed you could make that vision a reality. If you wrote *true* next to statement four, then you had some basis for your dreams other than self-will and self-determination. Children who grow up believing that God is not only all-powerful and all-knowing but that he also takes a personal interest in each of his children's welfare have the advantage of trusting in something greater than themselves for their "plans to be established." This doesn't mean that people like me, who didn't come to believe this until later in life, cannot achieve their goals as well as those who grow up trusting God at a young age. God just reaches us later on, when we're ready for him and for whatever plans he has laid out for us.

Proverbs 3:5 calls us to:

> Trust in the Lord with all your heart
> and lean not on your own understanding.

This verse implies that God has a plan for our lives and that we would do well to seek his guidance rather than relying on our own volition. Believing that God has an interest in our personal lives and development is essential to following the thread that ties this book together. When we stop relying on ourselves and turn to God, we can begin to forgive ourselves for our mistakes and failings, such as neglecting our gifts and talents.

I did not learn what it meant to have an intimate and personal relationship with God until I was in my mid-thirties. It wasn't until then that I really started to learn what Scripture had to say about trusting in God and not leaning on my own understanding. Once the truth of that sank in and I started relying on God and not myself, my life changed dramatically. I began to see my writing as a pathway to a closer relationship with God, not as a glorification of myself. I began to trust him for inspiration and guidance. I quit berating myself about not starting sooner and instead praised God every day that he was opening my eyes to how I could use the talent he gave me to bring my life into proper alignment with his will. I began to see writing as a way to glorify him. I learned to forgive the discouragers in my life and began to see God as my most important encourager.

God is calling "all who are skilled among you...to come and make everything [he] has commanded" (Exodus 35:10). Even if out of fear, stubbornness, or rebelliousness we have chosen (and perhaps are still choosing) not to trust God and obey him, we should not allow that fact to be another reason to feel discouraged about ourselves. Just as the father, joyful at the return of his prodigal son, forgave him for squandering his inheritance, so our heavenly Father will welcome us back whenever we ask forgiveness for ignoring his presence with us in the past (Luke 15:11-32). As we will see in the next chapter, God has given us the Holy Spirit through whom we can come to understand and live the meaningful life God has designed for us. God invites us to use our gifts and talents to become cocreators with him.

As artists blessed with God-given talents, we are fortunate indeed because these talents provide a very clear indication of what our lives, at least in part, should look like. If we have been given artistic gifts, the shape of our lives needs to include the use of those gifts. God's gifts are no accident: "Every good and perfect gift is from above, coming down from the Father of the heavenly lights, who does not change like shifting shadows" (James 1:17). The Lord is our greatest encourager. With our hand firmly planted in his, we can relearn the childlike trust we need to develop a vision of who he wants us to be. Proverbs 16:3 tells us, "Commit your works to the LORD and your plans will be established" (NASB). An important initial step in committing our works to the Lord is to forgive ourselves for not doing so to begin with. The next step is to move on and not look back.

THE FREEDOM OF FORGIVENESS

By now it should be apparent that identifying where our discouragement origi-
nated is not nearly as important as freeing ourselves from the effects of that discouragement. We can only do this by practicing the forgiveness that sets us free.
If we want to regain or give birth to a new vision for our lives as creative, productive artists, we must first let go of the past. On the following page is a famous
prayer that is worth memorizing. It can encourage you to become an instrument
of the Lord's peace through the act of forgiveness.

EXERCISE 5: ACT OF CONTRITION

In the Roman Catholic Church, the Act of Contrition (see page 178)
is a prayer of confession and a request for forgiveness. In this box or
in your artist's daybook, write a prayer asking for forgiveness for not
trusting your dreams and visions to "the Father of the heavenly lights."
End your prayer with a firm resolve to begin to seek God's vision for
you and to trust in his ability to help you achieve that vision.

A Prayer of Contrition

_____

_____

_____

_____

_____

_____

_____

_____

The Prayer of St. Francis of Assisi

Lord, make me an instrument of thy peace.

Where there is hatred, let me sow love; where there is injury, pardon;

Where there is discord, union; where there is doubt, faith;

Where there is despair, hope;

Where there is darkness, light; where there is sadness, joy.

Grant that we may not so much seek to be consoled as to console;

To be loved as to love.

For it is in giving that we receive;

It is in pardoning that we are pardoned;

And it is in dying that we are born to eternal life.

A sweet relief comes when we lay aside the mantle of judgment and allow ourselves to forgive. St. Francis's prayer is an invitation to take hold of the peace that surpasses all understanding; we can know that peace when we free ourselves from the burden of resentment. Forgiveness in one of the most powerful tools we can use as we continue to follow our creative call.

Do not judge, and you will not be judged.
Do not condemn, and you will not be condemned.
Forgive, and you will be forgiven.

—LUKE 6:37

CHAPTER FIVE

BREATHING IN

*But it is the spirit in a man, the breath of the Almighty,
that gives him understanding.*

JOB 32:8

*I*n ancient Greek mythology a Muse was one of nine beautiful young nymphs who presided over and inspired all great work in the arts and sciences. Artists would honor the Muse and pray for inspiration, without which, they believed, all creative efforts were in vain. When the classical poet Homer (c. 850 B.C.), author of *The Iliad* and *The Odyssey,* went to the page to compose one of his great epics, he would invoke Clio, the muse of history, and Calliope, muse of epic poetry and rhetoric. *The Iliad* begins, "Sing, O Muse!" calling upon something greater than the poet to "sing" into his mind and give spirit to his words. Invoking the Muse meant praying for inspiration to create. Even before the time of Christ, there was a recognition that creativity sprang from a source outside of and greater than the artist.

MUSING ON THE MUSE

In the Greek tragedy *The Trojan Women* (first performed in 416 B.C.), the playwright Euripides gave his chorus this doleful invocation:

> Sing me, O Muse, a song for Troy,
>
> a strange song sung to tears,
>
> a music for the grave.
>
> O lips, sound forth a melody for Troy.

The chorus voices the idea that the song and the music come through the lips of the performers, having passed through the pen of the playwright, but always originating with the Muse. Similarly, in Aeschylus's *Agamemnon,* a tragedy that also deals with the aftermath of the Trojan War, the chorus speaks these lines:

> Power is mine to sing of a journey of heroes, fate-driven.
>
> Old though we are, the spirit of God
>
> Breathes in us music's mighty persuasion.

The "spirit of God," through the poet's gift, infuses the chorus with "music's mighty persuasion." (The word *music* literally means "the art of the Muses.")

The Greeks of the fourth and fifth centuries B.C. were, for the most part, polytheists; however, among the many gods they worshiped was one they referred to only as the "Unknown God." They were, therefore, quite ready for Christianity when Paul brought it to them in the first century A.D. Some Greeks saw Jesus as their long-awaited "Unknown God." These people converted to the new religion, leaving their gods, demigods, and heroes to survive only in beautiful fables, or *myths,* from the word *mythos* meaning "story." Today, the old religion is long gone. What remains from those ancient people is their science, their architecture, their art, their philosophy, their concept of democracy, and their literature, all of which, they believed, were inspired by some source outside themselves, whom they called the Muse.

By 1674, when John Milton wrote *Paradise Lost,* the idea of a beautiful young nymph inspiring a poet had passed into a quaint classical ideal in the collective consciousness of the western world. What had replaced it, for Christians, was a belief in the Holy Spirit as the artist's Muse: the source of inspiration, more powerful than the artist and quite separate from him or her. Read these words from Book I of *Paradise Lost,* Milton's invocation of the Holy Spirit as Muse, as he begins his epic poem about the fall of Adam and Eve (I have changed the wording slightly for clarity):

> Sing, Heav'nly Muse… I now
> Invoke thine aid…
> Thou, O Spirit, that does prefer
> Before all Temples the pure and upright heart,
> Instruct me, for Thou knowest; Thou from the first
> Was present, and, with mighty wings outspread,
> Dovelike sat brooding on the vast Abyss…
> What is dark in me
> Illumine; what is low, raise and support.

Milton's "Heav'nly Muse" is clearly the Holy Spirit, the "Spirit that…prefer[s] before all Temples the pure and upright heart," who "from the first was present, and, with mighty wings outspread" brooded over all creation. This imagery owes much to Genesis 1:2: "Now the earth was formless and empty, darkness was over the surface of the deep, and the Spirit of God was hovering over the waters." God's Holy Spirit was hovering over the waters of chaos, brooding over the empty abyss. And out of his omnipotence, out of the depths of his own Spirit, God speaks what are arguably the four most important words in creation: "Let there be light." And, we are told, there was light.

This is the same Spirit that Milton called on to enlighten him, the same Spirit we call on today to inspire us, as artists, to become cocreators with God. Calling on the Holy Spirit is what Milton meant when he invoked the Muse, and that is what I mean throughout this book. God has given us our talents, and the Holy Spirit, when called on, will breathe his life into us so that we will know what to do with those talents. The Spirit of God is working in us whether or not we are aware of it, but when we consciously choose, with a "pure and upright heart," to invoke his aid, we can expect that he will "illumine…raise and support" us. With God's Spirit working in us, we can speak the words he gives us (in whatever artist language we use to express ourselves) and become cocreators with him. That is what being a Christian artist means: Our art is not necessarily Christian in content, but it is centered in the truth that the Holy Spirit reveals.

 We have not received the spirit of the world but the Spirit who is from God, that we may understand what God has freely given us.

—1 CORINTHIANS 2:12

The prayer on the next page will be familiar to Catholics, Episcopalians, and Anglicans. It can be found in both the Catholic *Missal* and the Episcopalian *Book of Common Prayer.*

EXERCISE 1: INVOCATION OF THE HOLY SPIRIT

Using the prayer to the Holy Spirit on page 73 as a model or employing a form of your own, write a personal invocation to the Holy Spirit. The purpose of this prayer will be to call forth his creative, enlightening power whenever you begin to create, just as the classical writers did. The prayer should also remind you to offer yourself as a servant to the artist work God wants you to do. This will be your Artist Prayer, which you can use to get started, to keep going, and to get past the inevitable blocks as you pursue your art.

Come, Holy Spirit, fill the hearts of thy faithful
And enkindle them with the fire of thy love;
Send forth thy spirit, and they shall be created,
And Thou shalt renew the face of the earth.

I like this prayer and still say it whenever I need inspiration, counsel, or wisdom. The language may seem a little bit stiff and old-fashioned, so it might not be as meaningful to everyone. But like the great poets of old, each of us should compose our own personal invocation or prayer for inspiration. Let's get right to our first exercise for this chapter: writing our own Invocation of the Holy Spirit.

THE CREATOR, THE SPIRIT, AND THE WORD

The mystery of the Trinity is just that—a mystery. Sometimes I think that the more we try to separate and differentiate the three persons of God, the more befuddled we become. But as I've started to view my creative development as a spiritual issue, I've begun to see the creation stories in both Genesis 1 and John 1 as metaphors for the creative process. I see God the Father as the Artist or Creator, Jesus as the expression of God's creativity, and the Holy Spirit as the source of inspiration for that which is created. See if you can follow my reasoning as we go through a few examples of important creation stories in the Bible.

In the beginning, we are told in Genesis, "the earth was formless and empty, darkness was over the surface of the deep, and the Spirit of God was over the waters" (1:2). The Spirit of God was suspended over the dark waters of chaos, brooding in expectation until the darkness was conquered by God's words: "Let there be light!" And so the process of creation began. Which came first, the inspiration or the act of creation? It doesn't matter. They were both present from the beginning. Furthermore, that creative process included not only the

Father-creator and the Spirit-inspirer, but also the Son, who, John tells us, was with God "from the beginning."

"In the beginning was the Word, and the Word was with God, and the Word was God. He was with God in the beginning" (John 1:1-2). If this is true, then in what capacity was Jesus "with God in the beginning"? John tells us. Jesus was "the Word." "Through [Jesus] all things were made; without him nothing was made that has been made" (John 1:3). Clearly, then, Jesus was present at the creation of the world, and John refers to him as "the Word." If we go back to Genesis again, we see three elements that were present—the Spirit of God, God the Creator, and the words God spoke. After the words were spoken, light was created, but before the light came the words. This is why I think John refers to Jesus as "the Word." Those three elements—God, Spirit, and Son as Creator, Inspiration, and Medium of expression (words)—were present "in the beginning."

As we more deeply heed the creative call and accept more fully God's invitation to become cocreators with him, we will see that these three elements of the creative process must be present for creativity to occur in our artist lives: creator (artist), inspiration (the Spirit), and medium of expression (our creative language). Recognizing that our own creative production mimics divine creation as set forth in both the Old and New Testaments may help us become aware of the connection between our artistic talents and God, the Great Artist.

The Word became flesh and made his dwelling among us.

—JOHN 1:14

When Jesus' cousin John baptized Jesus in the Jordan, all three persons of the Trinity were present again. In Mark 1:10-11 we read: "As Jesus was coming up out of the water, he saw heaven being torn open and the Spirit descending on him like a dove. And a voice came from heaven: 'You are my Son, whom I love; with you I am well pleased.'" The Spirit appears as a dove, but not a dove that floats gently and silently onto the scene: the heavens were "torn open." (Birth, after all, is a wrenching experience.) After the Spirit appears, we hear the voice of God who speaks the words that "inspire" Jesus as he begins his ministry on earth: "You are my Son, whom I love; with you I am well pleased." Once again, we see the three elements of the creative process: Creator, Spirit, and Word—Word as manifested both in a voice and in the Son. God the Father, God the Holy Spirit, and God the Son. Artist, inspiration, and expression—all present. Creation is again the result: Something new—the new covenant, the new ministry of Jesus—is born.

See, I am doing a new thing! Now it springs up; do you not perceive it?
—ISAIAH 43:19

The creative process as a cycle—artist, inspiration, expression, creation—is seen again in another passage in the Bible. At Pentecost the Holy Spirit appeared in an even more spectacular way. The followers of Jesus were gathered together, dispirited and directionless after Jesus' death. They had lost the vision that had been the focus of their lives for the past three years. Then, exactly what Jesus had promised happened:

> Suddenly a sound like the blowing of a violent wind came from
> heaven and filled the whole house where they were sitting. They saw
> what seemed to be tongues of fire that separated and came to rest on
> each of them. All of them were filled with the Holy Spirit and began
> to speak in other tongues as the Spirit enabled them. (Acts 2:2-4)

Luke, the author of Acts, tells us that the apostles spoke in "other tongues" after receiving this infusion of inspiration. Many translations of Acts use the phrase "other languages" rather than "other tongues." The apostles were empowered to speak the good news of salvation through Jesus Christ to people of all nations and cultures. With this scene in mind, let's take a look at how the story of Pentecost might relate to the artist today.

Two important metaphors for the artist are the images of the Holy Spirit as wind and as fire. Those elemental forces, which can carve a Grand Canyon and melt mountains, symbolize the power that begins to work in us when we invite the Holy Spirit into our lives. Madeleine L'Engle writes, "The Holy Spirit calls forth from us all that is nurturing and intuitive. The wind of the Spirit can be balmy and tender, but it can also be fierce, can lash waves to mountainous heights, can become a tornado which creates destruction in its path."[1]

The Holy Spirit is also depicted as "tongues of fire that separated and came to rest on each of [the disciples]" (Acts 2:3). For today's artist there may be another way to look at this *gift of tongues.* As we have already seen, usually when the Holy Spirit manifests itself to the world, the Holy Spirit "moves" and then God "speaks." It is by the combination of moving and speaking that creation occurs. Could "the sound like the blowing of a violent wind [that] came from heaven and filled the whole house where [the disciples] were sitting" be the inspiration of the Holy Spirit which the artist experiences? Could the tongues of fire that gave the apostles the power to speak the gospel in all languages represent for us the empowerment to "speak" our art to the world as a way of expressing whatever God wants our art to express?

If we look at the story of Pentecost this way, we can cast off anxiety about where our ideas and inspiration will come from. When we accept the Lord Jesus into our lives, we receive the indwelling of the Holy Spirit. Folk artist Howard Finster tells it this way: "The Holy Spirit came into my life and lifted my soul up and made a new person out of me.... That was the greatest thing that happened in all the days of my life.... I had been born to the Holy Ghost, the Holy Spirit of God. And that is still with me now, and I am over eighty years old. It will never leave me, that feeling of the Holy Ghost."[2] When we welcome the Holy Spirit into our lives, we are changed, and our art manifests that change.

THE BREATH OF HEAVEN

The word *spirit* and the word *breath* are the same in many languages, including Sanskrit *(pragna)*, Hebrew *(ruach)*, Latin *(spiritus)*, and Greek *(pneuma)*. The Latin root for both *spirit* and *inspire* is the word *spiritus*, meaning *breath. Inspire* means "to breathe into" (*in,* into + *spirare,* to breathe).

> *The most beautiful and profound emotion we can experience is the sensation of the mystical. It is the sower of all true science. He to whom this emotion is a stranger, who can no longer wonder and stand rapt in awe, is good as dead.*
>
> —ALBERT EINSTEIN

Second Timothy 3:16 begins, "All Scripture is inspired by God" (RSV). The word that is translated here as "inspired by God" is *theopneustos,* which literally means "God-breathed" in the Greek. To receive inspiration means "to breathe in the spirit." Inspiration is God's breath taken into ourselves. God wants to breathe his creative life into us through the inspiration of the Holy Spirit. We need simply to accept the gift.

E. M. Forster writes, "In the creative state a man is taken out of himself. He lets down, as it were, a bucket into his subconscious, and draws up something

EXERCISE 2: QUICKWRITE

In your daybook write for ten minutes without pausing. List everything that inspires you, that breathes life into you, that kindles the creative fires.

Choose one or two and describe these special inspirational sources in detail. What makes them so powerful to you?

that is normally beyond his reach. He mixes this thing with his normal experiences and out of the mixture he makes a work of art." This observation is one of those statements that may elicit an "if only it were always true" sigh from the reader. When we as Christian artists drop that metaphorical bucket down into our subconscious minds, we sometimes come up empty. The trick is to practice dropping our reliance on ourselves as the source of inspiration and instead to call upon the Holy Spirit as our muse. We have to realize, however, that just as God doesn't always answer our prayers when and how we think he should, he doesn't send us great, inspired artistic ideas on demand either. Sometimes we're called to simply wait.

What we call *artist's block* often stems from reliance on oneself as a source of ideas and energy apart from our reliance on the Holy Spirit. I believe that when artists seek the inspiration of the Holy Spirit, the breath of God stirs within them and God reveals what they are to do and how they are to do it. Of course our own humanness can get in the way; pressures from deadlines, fear of failure, and physical or mental exhaustion can all be barriers to receiving inspiration. One could even argue that, as James tells us, we should "consider it pure joy…whenever you face trials of many kinds, because you know that the testing of your faith develops

EXERCISE 3: OUT OF THE BLUE

Where do you get your creative ideas? Is there a certain place or a certain activity that seems to provide the right conditions for ideas to come to you? Does it happen while you sleep? In the car? While walking or showering? Write in your daybook about a time when you received an inspiration "out of the blue." If you can't think of a specific instance, write about the time, place, and conditions that seem to be most conducive to the "Aha!" experience.

perseverance. Perseverance must finish its work so that you may be mature and complete, not lacking anything" (1:2-4). When we learn to call first upon the inspiration of the Holy Spirit in those dry times and then to wait in *elpizo,* "confident expectation," God *will* be faithful in his own time—and what he has for us will be worth the wait. "When God reveals Himself, when He inspires us, it is to say, *I will last, my Spirit will last; when my Spirit is within you what you do will be lasting.*"[3] That's worth waiting out a dry spell for, don't you think?

THE COURAGE TO CREATE

In chapter 4, we looked at the root of the word *encouragement* and found it had to do with "giving heart to" or "heartening" someone. Just as encouragement from people gives life (heart) to our efforts, inspiration gives purpose and direction (breath) to our art. This week, try to focus on two main ideas:

1. paying attention
2. making time to breathe in the inspiration God offers you

It takes courage to create, and we all need encouragement to become more creative. As we begin calling ourselves *artists,* owning the title *actor, painter, singer, sculptor, photographer,* or *writer* and not merely thinking of ourselves as people who do that kind of thing as a hobby (even if we do!), we will find that all of life offers us the stimulus to create. Once I began calling myself a writer, I found that everywhere I went I found stories that needed to be written. But getting up the courage to actually refer to myself as a writer was difficult.

Is this true for you? Do you feel almost embarrassed to refer to yourself as an artist, as though you haven't earned the title yet? This reluctance is normal but is something we need to overcome. Once we do, we will start thinking as artists think. And once we begin to name ourselves *artists,* we begin to pay attention the way an artist does.

Anne Lamott, who calls herself "a writer who is a Christian" rather than "a Christian writer," observes, "There is ecstasy in paying attention. You can get into a kind of Wordsworthian openness to the world, where you see in everything the essence of holiness, a sign that God is implicit in all of creation…to see everything as an outward and visible sign of inward, invisible grace."[4]

In order to take in, to breathe in, the inspiration God offers us, we have to learn to pay attention to the world around us. Some artists refer to this as "filling the well" or "stocking the pond." Natalie Goldberg calls it "composting"—accumulating experiences and letting them ripen into the rich soil from which our art can bloom. Whatever you call the process, it's an approach to life born of a practice. The practice involves using your time, wherever you are, to take in what Marshall Cook calls a "healthy diet of sense impression. We must absorb the world around us and learn to see that world anew with eyes of childlike wonder. If we don't, when we try to describe, we'll have nothing but the words others have given us."[5]

BREATHING EXERCISES

Do you take time on a weekly basis to do something that stimulates your senses and feeds the artist within you? Do you make time to practice taking in the world around you? Most of us do not. The busyness of life keeps us from enjoying the luxury of taking ourselves to a movie, a play, an art museum, the library (simply to browse through the stacks, not to do research), the park, the beach, or wherever we can become recharged, energized, and, yes, inspired. Julia Cameron calls this "the artist date."[6] I call it *breathing exercises.*

My favorite breathing exercise is a visit to a little art museum here in my hometown that houses the world's largest collection of stained-glass windows and other beautiful objects by Louis Comfort Tiffany. The visual beauty of the windows, the cool quiet of the museum, the feeling of holiness in the reconstructed chapel housed within the museum's walls all feed my spirit and lift me up. I leave feeling revitalized and inspired.

Where do you like to go to nourish your creative self? When was the last time you took yourself there just for the beauty of it?

Exercise 4: "If only...I would..."

Fill in each of the following blanks as many ways as you want. (You may want to use this as a daybook entry so you will have more space.)

"If time and money were not an object, I would take myself to...

_____

_____

"If time and money were not an object, I would buy myself...

_____

_____

"If time and money were not an object, I would learn how to...

_____

_____

"If time and money were not an object, I would give myself the gift of...

_____

_____

"If time and money were not an object, I would give someone I love...

_____

_____

The list you just made can be a springboard for thinking about places to go and things to do to feed your artist self the raw materials of creativity. Exercises like this also allow you to practice thinking in terms of possibilities. Often when we stop to think about the things we would like to do, we realize that time and money are not as much of an impediment as we first thought. Choose one breathing exercise you really *can* find an hour or so to do and do it. If you are in a group, be prepared to tell your group about your experience. Talk about how you felt and about any resistance, external or internal, you may have encountered in making and following through on your plans. Whether or not you are in a group, write about the experience in your daybook either while you are experiencing it (I take my daybook with me whenever I'm doing breathing exercises) or afterwards.

Take a Breather, Not a Guilt Trip

Many people feel guilty about leaving spouses, children, or friends to go off by themselves just to "take a breather." I have heard people say that it is hard enough to find the time to go out with their partner, much less to go off all by themselves. Isn't taking oneself out a bit self-indulgent? Besides, some people believe that going off alone somewhere couldn't be much fun. Wouldn't it be kind of sad if you were to see, hear, feel, taste, smell, or experience something extraordinary and not have someone to share it with you? Well, no. In fact, sharing that extraordinary experience—that inspiration—can weaken it. Let me explain.

Although some people need to talk through their plans before they do them, many of us lose our momentum when we talk about what we want to do instead of just going ahead and doing it. The energy that could go into creating something artistic as a result of the stimulus we've just experienced or the idea we've just received can be defused by discussing it with someone else. "Words to the heat of deeds cold breath gives," says Macbeth as he tells himself to quit talking and start *doing* what he's deliberating about. He needs to act before his desire to do so cools. Shakespeare knew that for many people, talking about "deeds" we plan to do blows "cold breath" on our resolve to do them.

This is not to say that we should sequester ourselves from the rest of the world (at least not all the time!). There is certainly a kind of energy we can get from interacting with other people. The Holy Spirit will often speak through someone who is close to us, and there is a real place in the artist's life for small groups, classroom experiences, and intimate friendships.

> *I am the LORD your God, who brought you up out of Egypt. Open wide your mouth and I will fill it.*
>
> —PSALM 81:10

All that I am proposing is that you make an appointment with yourself to do something that might recharge your artistic batteries and to do it alone, even if it is just for one hour a week. That is what breathing exercises are all about: taking time to be alone, to absorb whatever God wants you to take in. When you give the artist within you this kind of quality time, you will have more to offer the people you love when you are with them.

I know that if you are a single parent or are in a time of your life where you don't feel as though you have a minute—or a dollar—to spare, one hour a week may seem like a luxury you just can't afford. There are ways to work around this, however, if you really want to start being a more artistic person. For instance, if you have young kids at home, you could trade babysitting services with another parent and then go to a free museum, art exhibit, or lecture in town. Once you really focus on finding the time to do your breathing exercises, that time will become available. I have found that anyone who absolutely has no way to find an hour to themselves every week is either not trying hard enough or just doesn't have the time to devote to artistic renewal at all. But don't give up yet. Chapter 7 is all about making time for your art. You may come across a key or two in that chapter for making your breathing exercises a weekly priority.

However you carve out the time, I can't stress enough how important it is that you breathe in the stuff that your art is made of. You can only do that if you start taking the time to do some of your favorite things.

EXERCISE 5: PLAYING FAVORITES

For your final exercise in this chapter, make a list of your favorites: people, places, foods, music, colors, seasons, holidays, animals, things to do, sights, sounds, tastes, and smells.

_____

_____

_____

_____

_____

_____

Next, go through magazines, boxes of photographs, collections of things you have saved because you like them. Get out markers, crayons, paints, glitter, orphan earrings, buttons, stickers, or whatever you have. Take a piece of poster board and make a mixed-media collage illustrating a few of your favorite things. Hang it in your artist workspace. Look at it whenever you need ideas about where to go for your breathing exercises.

"Out with the Bad Air, in with the Good"

We've defined "breathing exercises" as putting ourselves into places and positions where we can feed our sensory receptors and open our hearts to the inspiration of the Holy Spirit. Another technique for becoming open to "such stuff as dreams are made on," (from Shakespeare's *The Tempest*—and, yes, surprisingly enough it is "on" and not "of") involves *being specific about what you'd like to produce.* Whatever you're trying to produce, saturate yourself with that genre. If you're writing poetry, read all the poetry you can. If you're designing a dance, go to dance rehearsals and observe, write down what you see, take in sensory impressions. If you're painting, go to art galleries, look at books that contain the same kind of painting you're working on, or observe a local painting class. My friend Jackie has a plaque on the wall of her office that reads, "What you focus on expands." By pinpointing what it is you want from the Holy Spirit, you are more likely to get it and to recognize it for what it is when it actually comes. Write your goal down and carry it with you, reminding yourself throughout the day what your subconscious mind's assignment is. Then ask God to fill you with the inspiration you need to do it.

TAKING DOWN WHAT YOU'RE BREATHING IN

Marshall Cook, writer and creativity teacher, advises students to write down insights and inspirations just as they come, without trying to shape them too much. When you get a dream at night, try waking up just enough to write down whatever you can. Cook says that sometimes it turns out to be gibberish, but "I've also received the occasional precious gift from the muse…and these gifts make all the scribblings worth the effort."[7] Thinking of yourself as an artist, you'll develop artist habits, like keeping a notebook or sketchbook with you at all times. Develop the habit of writing down what you're breathing in.

Writer and news commentator Earl Nightingale writes, "Ideas are elusive, slippery things. Best to keep a pad of paper and a pencil at your bedside, so you can stab them during the night before they get away." As you grow comfortable thinking of yourself as an artist, you will want to have a notebook, sketchbook, or tape recorder with you almost everywhere you go. We never know when the Spirit will send us a message we'll want to remember later on.

God wants us to ask him for good gifts, and he wants us to be specific about what we want and need from him. If we train ourselves to be ready for the inspiration of the Holy Spirit by waiting in humble expectation, if we pay attention to the inspiration that is coming to us, and if we plan into our busy lives time to take in sensory fodder to feed our creativity, we will be on our way to becoming the artists God created us to be.

May the God of hope fill you with all joy
and peace as you trust in him,
so that you may overflow with hope
by the power of the Holy Spirit.
—ROMANS 15:13

CHAPTER SIX

BREATHING OUT

Commit your works to the LORD and your plans will be established.

PROVERBS 16:3, NASB

*B*y now writing in your daybook has become a habit. (Well, maybe thinking about writing in your daybook has become a habit.) You have worked through or are continuing to work through forgiving the discouragers in your life, you've started practicing your breathing exercises, and you are opening up to becoming available to the inspiration of the Holy Spirit. But now that you are ready to start on the production phase of the creative process, everything in the world starts getting in the way. Your spouse is having a bad time at work and needs to talk when he or she gets home at night. Your son gets sick. School projects are due, and your daughter needs your help. You decide to download a newer version of your Web browser and your computer crashes. You take on a new responsibility at work or at your kids' school or caring for your parents, and there goes the little bit of free artist time you thought you had. What's going on here? Is the universe conspiring to keep you from doing your art? Is it the universe, or is it fear of flying?

No amount of preparation can completely allay the fears that immobilize us when we finally set about the task of engaging in creative work. These very activities, which are at the top of our "things I like to do in my spare time" list, can seem formidable when we confront the empty canvas, the blank page, the blinking cursor, the new piece of sheet music. I almost always experience a point where I'm holding my breath, afraid to start. In fact, I avoided starting this chapter for weeks before I could force myself to begin. Something about knowing I was going to write about getting down to the business of creating kept me from getting down to the business of creating! I'd spend hours searching the Internet, revising previous chapters, working on submissions to publishers, anything to postpone beginning to actually write about beginning to actually write. What I needed to do was to get down to work, to start writing, to quit holding my breath, and to start breathing out.

Once I quit doing my avoidance dance and started typing, the words began to flow and the inspiration began to come. I needed to begin writing *before* I knew exactly what I was supposed to write. In the act of creating I was shown that *we create by becoming servants to the work.*

SERVING THE WORK

In order to practice our art—to breathe out what God wants us to express through the talents he has given us—we must become servants to the work. Servants *do;* servants *act.* Madeleine L'Engle has written extensively on this idea: "The artist must be obedient to the work.... Each work of art, whether it is a work of great genius or something very small, comes to the artist and says, 'Here I am. Enflesh me. Give birth to me.' And the artist either says, 'My soul doth magnify the Lord,' and willingly becomes the bearer of the work, or refuses."[1] God wants us to put ourselves into his hands and say, "Lord, make me your servant. Teach me to use the talent you have given me to bring this work of art into being."

When we become servants of the work, we adopt an attitude that puts us in the ready position for the creativity to flow through us. We don't wait until we feel like starting, until we feel inspired, until we're excited and energized by the project. We make up our minds that, just as in any job we are paid to do, we will attend to the work at hand. We will show up at the easel, the blank canvas, the piano, the computer, the studio, not only when we are infused with ideas and energy, but also when we are not. "It's simple," says artist Jasper Johns. "You just take something and do something to it, and then do something else to it. Keep doing this, and pretty soon you've got something." The operative word is *doing*. We produce works of art by setting a time for creative work, by doing whatever exercises will prime our creative pump, by paying attention, and by being ready when the inspiration comes. We "breathe out" and start to make things.

Exercise 1: Scheduling Artist Time

This chapter is about serving the work, so let's schedule some blocks of artist time so we can do that. Whether it's daily, three times a week, or just once a week for starters, make sure the time you set aside is reasonable and conducive to attending to your artist work. Schedule this time just as you would an exercise class or a favorite TV show and then stick to it.

Once you develop the habit of working for specific periods of time, you may be able to stretch them out into longer blocks. Pray God's blessing on your efforts to develop this habit and record in your daybook how you do with keeping to the schedule this week.

I will work on my art every _____ from _____ to _____.

(signature) _____ (date) _____

In her book *Wild Mind: Living the Writer's Life,* writer and painter Natalie Goldberg puts it this way: "Sometimes people say to me, 'I want to write, but I have five kids, a full-time job…' I say to them, 'There is no excuse. If you want to write, write. This is your life. You are responsible for it. You will not live forever. Don't wait. Make the time now, even if it is ten minutes a week.'"[2] The habit of writing in your daybook proves that it *is* possible for you to make time for yourself and your art.

It is within my power either to serve God or not to serve Him. Serving Him, I add to my own good and the good of the whole world. Not serving Him, I forfeit my own good and deprive the world of that good which was in my power to create.

—LEO TOLSTOY

In the next chapter we will take a more in-depth look at making and protecting our designated artist time. In this chapter we will start digging in—getting out the clay, the pen and paper, the flute, the drawing board, the camera, the garden gloves, whatever tools we need to make ourselves available for God's creative energy to come through us. We'll do it by placing ourselves at the ready and paying attention to what starts to flow through us. And don't say, "Okay, I'll try." Remember what Yoda tells Luke Skywalker in the film *The Empire Strikes Back:* "Try? There is no try. There is only do or do not." Let's do, shall we?

MODELING CHILDLIKE BEHAVIOR

Most of us have heard about the psychotherapeutic concept of getting in touch with one's inner child. Creativity experts as well as psychologists invite us to look into our past in order to discover why we may have lost touch with that playful, inventive part of ourselves—why we may have stopped breathing out our artistic expression. It is possible that nothing traumatic or dramatic happened. It might simply be that as we grew up and looked to the adults around us for cues to healthy adult behavior, we didn't see people nurturing their creativity. What we did see were grown-ups who did grown-up things: working for a living, maintaining a home, taking care of others.

Without meaning to, adults who take no time for their artist selves teach their children not to take time for their artist selves either. We learn by observation that adulthood is about duty and responsibility, not about nurturing wonder and creativity. If adults model the practice of nurturing the artist within, their children will grow up believing that the road to adulthood doesn't have to be littered with castaway wonder, imagination, and the need to create.

Your Creator models appropriate adult behavior every minute of every day and night. Look around you at the works of his hands, the natural world that he created and is continually creating and recreating, and notice that he works creativity into every day of his eternal life. He wants to make us cocreators with him, but he can't do so unless we believe that doing the work of becoming an artist is important, so important that sometimes other things may not get done. Satan, the master of deception, tries to convince us that taking time to be an artist is selfish and even sinful. He will sometimes use our sensitivity to the needs of others to steal our artist time. He will do anything he can to prevent that sweet communion with our Creator. Don't listen to him. Doing artist work, when we let the Spirit lead us, is doing God's work.

WHAT'S SO HARD ABOUT GETTING STARTED?

Many of us treat doing our art as the least important item on our daily to-do list. We are trained from a very young age to believe that doing what we want to do should come only after we've done what we must do. We may believe on some subliminal level that writing or painting or playing music or whatever our talent urges us to do is a form of play, so it should only be done after we finish the "real" work of the day. This is one reason why many of us have such a hard time taking our art seriously: We tend to "work it in" rather than make it our work. God doesn't give us a talent and then neglect to give us the desire to develop it, to find it rewarding and enjoyable. Just because we enjoy practicing our art doesn't mean it isn't work and doesn't mean it isn't *meaningful* work.

The fact that practicing our art is enjoyable and satisfying is partly why we feel more complete when we are being creative. We want to do it because it feels good when we do; despite the work of it, we find the effort fulfilling and fun. We have to reprogram our minds to believe that the work of our artist selves is at least as important as the work of our housekeeper selves, our yard-maintenance selves, our parenting selves, and our workaday world selves. By allowing our artist self to blossom and grow, we will be enhancing all those other selves, including the part of us that cares for and nurtures others. Even though people who are used to getting a lot of us may balk at the idea that we now need more time to ourselves, they will ultimately be getting smaller doses of a higher quality *you* as you come into your own as an artist. Everyone around us will profit from the happier, calmer, more satisfied person each of us will grow to be.

We must get past the notion that if we like doing something, it should be a reward permitted only after we've completed the things we don't like doing. (If I were doing all the housekeeping and errand running I need to do right now, I wouldn't be writing this chapter!) If you get honest about it, writing, painting, singing, acting, composing music—all these activities require a great deal of work and practice, which isn't always "fun." Ask any child who is taking music lessons and has to practice before he can go out to play with his friends. Our inner children know that serving the art is rewarding work, but it *is* work.

One reason we see art as something other than true "work" is that we tend to view it in terms of result rather than process. If we paint murals for a living and are paid for our work, we can justify the time spent at that endeavor. But if we paint watercolors for the pure joy of creating something beautiful, we see that work as less worthy. We need to get over this idea that art needs to be marketable in order to be worthwhile.

FACING THE FEAR

In order to start breathing out regularly, we also have to overcome fear of failure. One reason artists become blocked is by using inertia to avoid feeling like losers. This behavior is all about self-protection, about playing it safe. No matter what your talent, all you have to do to avoid rejection is to never produce anything that could be rejected. Every day of my life I fight my tendency to avoid writing or piano practice, and I know why I do: I'm afraid. I'm afraid that if I finish the book or the poem or the musical composition, I'll have to put it out there where others will judge it. What if no one likes what I do? What if I never get anything published? What if I mess up when I play for other people?

What I have learned by pressing on past my fears is this: *When I acknowledge my fear, I deprive it of its power over me.* My friend and pastor John gave me this sage advice when I told him I was writing my first book: "Writing this book isn't about getting it published; it's about you and what God wants to do with you in your life." Franky Schaeffer writes in *Addicted to Mediocrity: 20th Century Christians and the Arts,* "Remember that as a creative person, the important thing is to create. Who sees what you make, where it goes and what it does is a secondary consideration; the first is to exercise the talent God has given you."[3]

Every time we hesitate to begin for fear of failing or seeming frivolous, we must fill that moment of hesitation with prayer. Then we must follow that prayer with action, with doing something, *anything* that will get us moving forward in the practice of our art. The musician might practice some simple piece he learned as a child or warm up with scales and arpeggios. The visual artist can go outside and do some quick sketches or throw some scraps of paper down and put together a simple collage. The artistic gardener goes out to the garden and

EXERCISE 2: WHAT ARE YOU AFRAID OF?

Circle the number before each fear that applies to you. Leave the lines beneath each statement blank for now.

1. Fear that my family life and social life will suffer if I spend time on my art

    _____

    _____

2. Fear that I'll seem self-indulgent to others if I schedule and protect my artist time

    _____

    _____

3. Fear that it will seem arrogant for me to think I can produce anything "good enough"

    _____

    _____

4. Fear of calling myself an artist

    _____

    _____

5. Fear of loneliness as friends assume that I'm too busy "acting like an artist" to do things with them

    _____

    _____

6. Fear of rejection if I submit my work for publication, exhibition, or sale

    _____

    _____

7. Fear of spending time and money on my art that ought to go to other more "responsible" things

_____

_____

8. Fear that I don't have enough talent

_____

_____

9. Fear that others will think I'm irresponsible

_____

_____

10. Fear that people I respect won't like what I produce

_____

_____

11. Fear of my own tendency to quit before I finish something

_____

_____

12. Fear that I'll be just adding another source of stress to my life

_____

_____

You may have thought about other fears as you worked through this exercise. Write about them in your next daybook entry. Right now, however, go back through and try to turn each of these fear statements into a positive statement. For example, you might write for number one, "My family relationships and friendships will be enhanced as I become a more complete person by my attending to my art." Post the affirmations you like best in your studio. If you're in a group, share the most helpful ones with your group.

decides, "I'm not going to try to redo this entire bed. I'm just going to deadhead the petunias." You get the idea. When we practice our art as servants to the work, whether the work is successful or not becomes secondary to the work God will be doing in us through that art. Franky Schaeffer makes no apology for what he sees as job one for artists: "Produce, produce, produce! Create, create, create! Work, work, work! That is what we must do as Christians in the arts...if we are to exercise our God-given talent, praise him through it, enjoy it, bear fruit in the age in which we live."[4]

Exercise 3 might help you when you're ready to get serious about the productive phase of your new artist life.

A SENSE OF SPACE

Having a specific place to practice your art is essential if you are serious about beginning to "breathe out" the talents you've been given. Artist spaces are as varied as artists themselves. I prefer to be alone with Celtic or classical music playing

EXERCISE 3: THE FAMILY CONTRACT

Work with members of your family in drawing up a contract that defines how they will grant you the time, space, and privacy you need to do your artist work. If you live alone, you might make a contract with *yourself* about what kinds of intrusions you will and will not allow during your artist time. Your contract should address phone-answering and door-answering issues. (I don't do either during my artist time.)

In my house it is now taken for granted that whenever I'm in my study with the door closed, I am off limits unless there is a real emergency. I do want my husband and son to come in and say good-bye softly in the background and a scented candle burning nearby. A cup of tea within my reach is comforting during my artist time. I find that even a small distraction like having to answer a question ("Do you know if we have any more of that leftover pasta?") can break my concentration while I am writing. Answering the phone can be deadly, which is why, I'm convinced, God created answering machines.

I am fortunate enough to live in a house that allows me a room of my own. I have furnished it with a garage-sale oak library table for my long-hand writing. A small kitchen table I no longer use in the kitchen is my computer "desk." An old twelve-drawer card catalog cabinet my school library was discarding holds my writing supplies. A couple of wooden file cabinets, a large bookcase, and some comfortable office chairs (also found at garage sales) make up the rest of the furnishings. I probably have no more than a couple hundred dollars invested in furnishing this sanctuary where I spend most of my creative time.

I love this room. The Florida afternoon sun slants through my collection of colored glass bottles, its reflection off the swimming pool outside my window

whenever they are leaving the house, and that's part of our agreement. I also don't like to have the door closed all the time, so I put up a sign when I want to work undisturbed. (In the next exercise you will be making your own Do Not Disturb sign. If you live alone, you can put that sign above your telephone so that you won't answer it while you're working on your art.)

Discuss the contract with the people in your household and have everyone sign it. Celebrate afterwards! Make this step in the development of your artist life a joyful occasion. If you live alone, invite some close friends over and have them sign it with you. This will give you some accountability—people outside your home who will check up on you and see if you're living up to your new commitment to your art.

turning the gray walls a shimmering aquamarine. A poster I picked up for free at a book fair reminds me in colorful calligraphy, "BE SILENT and KNOW that I AM GOD. The Lord Almighty is here among us. Psalm 46:10-11." This is my space, and I'm comfortable here.

You may recall how, as a young girl, Mary Englebreit told her mother she needed an art studio, and her mother cleared out a linen closet for her artist space. It doesn't take a five-bedroom house to make a place for you to do your artist work (well, maybe it does if, like my friend Joyce, you have triplets!). Some artists even prefer to have their studio right in the heart of the house where their family spends most of its time. Where you work is not as important as having a designated place to work. If you have children, part of your family contract needs to state that your supplies and studio space are off-limits to them, or else you'll never be able to find your materials when you need them. If a computer is a tool of your trade, you may have to think about buying a second one for yourself and letting your kids use the older one. Your computer is your paint box, and you may need to keep it for only you.

You have to carve out your space wherever it is comfortable for you to be, remembering that insisting on having a space of one's own is not selfish or self-centered. It's a necessity; you need a studio in order to be productive. You should also insist that no matter how cluttered and disorganized your studio space may seem to others, the other people living in your house do not have the right to add their stuff to your clutter. It's your clutter, by golly, and it's off limits to everyone else. Children and spouses are not allowed to take the scissors or the rubber cement from your studio. You don't want to go out to work on your bonsai collection and find your best pruning tools missing. When you go to practice your singing and your boom box with your practice tapes has been "borrowed," your might find yourself singing in octaves you never imagined you could reach! Provide a stockpile of supplies that your family is allowed to use and store that collection in another part of the house. Then give notice that whatever is in your studio is for your use only.

A Room of One's Own

Norcroft is a retreat center for women writers located on Lake Superior in Minnesota. Each woman lucky enough to be awarded a fellowship to go there not only has her own bedroom for the duration of her stay, but is also given a private writing cabin, overlooking the lake, where she can work all day undisturbed. The reason for Norcroft's very existence is the recognition that artists, especially women who always seem to be on call in the home as well as in the workplace, need solitude and space in order to be truly productive. Virginia Woolf, in her wonderful little book *A Room of One's Own,* makes the same point: "A woman [and I would add, "or a man"] must have money and a room of her own if she is to write."

EXERCISE 4: A PLACE FOR US

Where is your "bit of earth"? Where do you feel safest to create? Where in your home do you feel most at peace, least distracted? In your daybook, describe your ideal artist's studio. Where would it be? Would there be windows, and, if so, what would you see when you look out of them? What furniture, art pieces, memorabilia, photographs, and other accessories would you put in your studio? If you wish, draw a diagram or other illustration of this space.

If you already have a studio or work area, describe it. Is there anything you can do to make it more conducive to creative productivity? Sometimes just getting it uncluttered and better organized is all you need to make your space more workable.

Design and make a Do Not Disturb sign to hang on your door whenever you are working. Start using it. If you are in a group, bring it with you to your next meeting and share it with the other members.

Did you ever build a tree house or a fort out of old boxes or scraps of lumber when you were a kid? Ever throw sheets over a clothesline or a blanket over a couple of card tables and call it your clubhouse? What was so appealing about crawling into that special place and hanging out there all day long? By the afternoon, your fort (from the Latin root *fortis,* meaning "strong") might have been fully furnished. You would beg your parents to let you keep it up until the next day—and could you *please* sleep in it, just for tonight? Was creating your own space a self-centered act, or was it an expression of the need to claim, as Mary Lennox requests of her Uncle Archibald in *The Secret Garden,* a "bit of earth"? The need for a place all one's own runs deep within every artist.

BANISHING THE CRITIC

If inspiration is the breath of heaven, then the critic who sits on your shoulder and whispers discouraging words into your ear is its opposite. Inspiration comes from God, and the voice that tells us that what we are doing is not any good (will never sell, will never be published, is trivial, is lousy, is keeping us from our real responsibilities) comes right out of the pits of hell. Let's recognize this for what it is. Satan will try to confound and discourage us any way he can in order to keep us from actualizing our talents. One way he incapacitates us is by introducing the *critic* into the creative process.

The critic, the editor, the censor, the monitor, or whatever you choose to name it is that voice within that tells us everything that's not right about what we are working on. It is incapable of accepting the results of our efforts without criticism. To be sure, there is a place in the creative process for evaluation, and it's a poor artist who never edits, revises, or otherwise makes improvements and corrections. But at the early phase of the creative process, it is the artist's job to tell the critic that it has no place in one's studio or one's head. The great playwright Anton Chekov wrote in one of his letters, "You must once and for all give up being worried about successes and failures. Don't let that concern you. It's your duty to go on working steadily day by day, quite quietly, to be prepared for mistakes, which are inevitable, and for failures."

Be thankful that you have the power of prayer as you face those inevitable mistakes, disappointments, and failures. The critic wants you to worry about whether or not your work is "good enough." Since artists are never completely satisfied with their creations, if you listen to the critic you will become incapacitated and never create at all. *God is in control,* and every time you hear the critic telling you that you are wasting your time or being self-centered, you need to turn that message over to the Lord in prayer and rebuke the critic in the name of Jesus. You are fighting for your creative life here, and God is on your side.

Our relationship with God as our rescuer is the only healthy codependent relationship in this life. God wants you to turn to him; he wants to be your shield and your buckler. Pray Ephesians 6:14-18 for the full armor of protection. Then, safely within your fort, with guardian angels barring the door, you can relax and let the creative juices begin to flow.

Stand firm then, with the belt of truth buckled around your waist, with the breastplate of righteousness in place, and with your feet fitted with the readiness that comes from the gospel of peace. In addition to all this, take up the shield of faith, with which you can extinguish all the flaming arrows of the evil one. Take the helmet of salvation and the sword of the Spirit, which is the word of God. And pray in the Spirit on all occasions with all kinds of prayers and requests.

—EPHESIANS 6:14-18

When we stop worrying about the end result or final product, we free ourselves to become absorbed in the process and experience the joy of serving the work. It is ironic that when we adopt a servant attitude, which seems to imply bondage, we are actually set free to create something greater than ourselves, something that results from a collaboration between God and us. Is it any wonder the enemy strikes at our attempts to enter into this intimate relationship with our Creator?

Like the priests in the Old Testament, we bow before the altar and offer our sacrifice: our talent, our time, and our desire to enter into this incarnational union with God. Silence the critic. Call this invasion of your peace of mind what it is—an attack—and move into that communion with God that being an artist allows you to experience. Post these words from Isaiah somewhere in your studio: "This is what the LORD says—your Redeemer, the Holy One of Israel: 'I am the LORD your God, who teaches you what is best for you, who directs you in the way you should go'" (48:17). Read these words whenever you find yourself oppressed by the harassment of the critic. The critic, like the force of gravity, aims to bring us back to earth. Serving the work, breathing out, becoming the artist we were born to be is ethereal, heavenly work. Banish the critic that would keep you earthbound.

Take a minute to review some of the issues that creative people have to cope with in order to get down to the business of creative production:

- setting a specific time to do artistic work
- learning to protect creative time from outside demands
- claiming a space to do artist work
- banishing the critic

Which of these presents the biggest challenge for you?

_____

_____

Which one do you think you might have the most success overcoming?

_____

Make a special effort this week to work on overcoming the barrier you just identified. In order to achieve your creative goals, you must first *attend* to the work of being an artist. We will look at that idea next.

ATTENDING TO THE WORK

The word *attend,* according to the first definition in the *American Heritage College Dictionary,* means "to be present at" (for example, "to attend an opening or a concert"). This definition is reminiscent of Natalie Goldberg's admonition to writers that they "show up at the page." To *attend* is "to show up," to "be there." But a little farther on in this entry we find this definition: "to take care of; give attention to." Now we're getting somewhere.

When I attend to the work of being an artist, I am not merely showing up; I'm taking care of the work and giving attention to it. The third definition adds an even deeper meaning to the notion of attending to the work: "to apply or direct oneself." Ah! Applying ourselves or directing ourselves to the work—is this what I'm looking for? Close, but not quite. We have to go all the way to the fifth definition before we hit the mother lode: "to remain ready to serve; to wait." This is it.

Attending to the work is more than just showing up at the studio. It is more than focusing our attention on the work or applying and directing ourselves to the work. Attending to the work means "to remain *ready to serve; to wait.*" We attend to the work when we put ourselves, all our attention, at the service of that work, so that when the work calls to us, "Enflesh me!" we are poised to do that.

But how does this miraculous thing called "creating" happen? Do we just sit in our studio and wait for the Spirit to move us? Don't we need some kind of inspiration before we can speak the language of our art? Don't we, like the disciples at Pentecost, have to wait until the tongues of fire dance above our heads so that we are made capable of speaking out the truth through our art?

The answer is yes and no. Like the disciples, we have to place ourselves where the Spirit can meet us so that he can open our hearts and our mouths to speak out our "new thing." Had these disciples not been present, had they not attended that gathering with the other believers, they would have missed the opportunity to be a part of the birthing of the church. Had they been home doing the dishes or working at their "real" jobs, they might have been too preoccupied to receive the inspiration. Their attendance at Pentecost was accompanied by fear, doubt, and infighting, but nonetheless they were present where they were called to be present. They didn't receive the Holy Spirit and then start paying attention: They received the Holy Spirit because they were paying attention.

We must follow the disciples' example and write this on our minds and in our hearts: *Our talents and gifts are just as important as our ability to keep a family, a home, and a job running smoothly.* Always remember that our talents are gifts both to us and through us, and it is our responsibility to use them. Writers must write, musicians must play, painters must paint, weavers must weave, cooks must cook, and gardeners must garden whether they feel inspired at the moment or not. Sometimes just engaging in the humble work of putting shovel to soil is what it takes for a garden to be born.

Here is the most important thing you can take away from this chapter: *We cannot wait to be inspired before we start producing creatively.* Remember that at

---

EXERCISE 5: JUST DOING IT

I have a great poster by Fred Babb that says, "GO TO YOUR STUDIO AND MAKE STUFF." I keep it in the kitchen to remind me of what's important.

For the next thirty minutes (longer if you wish) do just that: Make stuff. Don't worry that you don't have a particular plan or outline. Simply keep your hand, your voice, or your body moving; don't even stop and think. See what comes of this small investment in time. Save whatever you produce (unless it is something to eat—if that's the case, invite a friend over and eat it!). Write about the experience in your daybook.

the creation of the world all three elements—the artist, the inspiration, and the expression—were there simultaneously. We must start producing, and, as we wait on the work, attend the work, serve the work through our own particular mode of artistic expression, we become open to the inspiration of the Holy Spirit in our art, in ourselves, and in our lives.

> *Whatever you do, work at it with all your heart, as working for the Lord.… It is the Lord Christ you are serving.*
>
> —COLOSSIANS 3:23-24

The work you are doing is more important than you may have realized because it's not just about being an artist. It is not just about using talents God has given you. It is about discipline and perseverance, about setting aside a specific time and place for attending to the work. It is about allowing perseverance to "finish its work so that you may be mature and complete, not lacking anything" (James 1:4). Commit yourself to serving the work, to waiting patiently for the Lord to reveal how he wants you to use your gifts by attending to the gifts he has given you. Begin with action, trusting God for the inspiration. Be courageous. Take heart that you are doing the work God created you to do.

> *Commend what you do to Yahweh,*
> *and what you plan will be achieved.*
>
> —PROVERBS 16:3, NJB

CHAPTER SEVEN

MAKING TIME

Always give yourselves fully to the work of the Lord,
because you know that your labor in the Lord is not in vain.

1 CORINTHIANS 15:58

I know I have talent, and I have more ideas for projects than I know what to do with. I just have too much going on in my life, and I can't imagine finding time to get into my art." I often hear these words, or some variation of them, when I tell people what this book is about. You might think that such statements would have clued me in to the importance of this chapter's subject and that I might have moved it to the beginning of the book. I *do* know how important making time for your art is: Lack of time is the single biggest impediment to people practicing their talents, and that's why this is the longest chapter in the book. I've saved it until near the end for a reason. Only when we know that developing our gifts is intimately related to our spiritual development and only when we've made the commitment to do something about that in our lives will we have the dedication to make the time we need to develop our art.

"TIME IS THE COIN OF YOUR LIFE"

We've all heard the adage, "Time is money." Reflecting as it does the Puritan work ethic by which most of us were raised, the saying has a ring of truth. This idea conditions us to believe that if time is money, the best use of our time is turning it *into* money. Of course we all need money to live, and God honors our desire to take responsibility for meeting that need. Unfortunately, the "time is money" mindset can lead us to spend our time making money at the expense of making art. It also fosters the belief that if our art can't make money, it isn't worth the time we invest in it.

> *You will never find time for anything. If you want time, you must make it.*
>
> —CHARLES BIXTON

If we pay prayerful attention to how we fill the minutes and hours of our days and if we critically examine the choices we make about how we spend our time—even if we have bills to pay, a house to maintain, or a family to care for—we will find that we *can* afford the time we need for our art.

EXERCISE 1: TIME BANDITS

When you try to visualize yourself taking time to practice your art, what other activities and responsibilities take precedence over your artistic endeavors? List the top three "time bandits" in your life right now.

_____

_____

_____

We can all glean some extra time each day to practice our art. If you spend twenty minutes with your daybook each morning and another thirty minutes practicing your art later in the day, you'll have spent less than one hour a day (the time it takes to watch one television program) developing your God-given talents. Can you find that fifty minutes? Do you believe God can help you find that time? Remember the scripture in the last chapter? Proverbs 16:3 says, "Commit your work unto the LORD, and your plans shall be established." This truth applies to our time as well as to the works of our hands.

Making time to be an artist is, as my husband is fond of saying, "more of a process than an event." Keep that in mind as you begin to say no to less important things in your life so you can say yes to your talents. Having time for your art won't happen overnight or simply because you have resolved to make it happen. There will be setbacks. You will find that making time is definitely a process that takes time.

In this chapter you will be evaluating your own time-management style and learning how to use that style to your advantage. You will take a look at how you actually use, spend, save, and waste time in your daily life, and you will be introduced to some ideas that will help you learn to make time for your art.

OPPOSITES ATTRACT

To be an artist we have to integrate the spontaneity of the child with the disciplined mind of the adult. Norman Podhoretz writes, "Creativity represents a miraculous coming together of the uninhibited energy of the child with its apparent opposite and enemy, the sense of order imposed on the disciplined adult intelligence." Like many artists, I struggle with that "sense of order imposed on the disciplined adult intelligence." Sometimes the only success I have with to-do lists, for example, is making one at the end of the day, writing down everything I actually did, then smiling smugly as I check each item off the list. I waste minutes that add up to hours looking for things that aren't where they belong, retracing steps because I forgot something, and getting off task by giving in to the many distractions that tempt me throughout my day. To make it worse, I'm a procrastinator who seems to be more motivated by pressure than by the pleasure of pacing myself. I'm pretty much a poster child for time-management dysfunction.

I used to spend a lot of time berating myself over how disorganized I was in my use of time. Like most extroverts, I am more motivated by external forces than internal ones. As long as I am on an externally imposed schedule, as I am on days when I teach, I accomplish a great deal. I nearly always feel a measure of satisfaction by day's end because, if nothing else, I've put in a good day's work with my students. The problem for me is how to manage my time after work, on weekends, and on days when I'm supposed to be writing.

I have recently gone from full-time to part-time work in order to have more time to write. It is not unusual on a writing day for me to firmly resolve when I first get out of bed to spend the rest of the morning working on my current project. But before I leave the kitchen with my first cup of coffee to head for my studio, I decide to wash up a few dishes. While I'm doing that, I'll notice that the compost bowl needs to be emptied. On my way outside to the compost heap, I'll stop to admire my flower garden in the pearly morning light, but I'll also see that it is nearly overrun by weeds. So I'll get my weeding fork from the garage to do a little garden maintenance, telling myself, "If I just do fifteen minutes now and another fifteen later, I'll get that flower bed looking great in no time. Besides, it's cool right now and this is good exercise."

Two hours later, I head back to the kitchen for a drink of water, but as I pass through the laundry room, I decide to start a load of wash before I go back outside. Of course, there is a wet load that needs to be moved to the dryer and a load in the dryer that needs to be folded and… Well, you get the picture. By the end of the day, I'll have started all kinds of chores and projects, completed only the ones I was really interested in, left a number of them half done, and found the morning dishes sitting in cold dishwater. Whatever happened to spending my morning writing? This kind of time management can be frustrating at best and debilitating at worst.

Until recently I thought that my hit-or-miss approach to life was a sign of character weakness, a lack of self-discipline and self-control. I believed that the reason I didn't have more time to spend practicing my writing or my music was because of a short attention span and poor follow-through skills. I was surprised to learn that recent brain-based research has revealed that this random way of approaching tasks is not a handicap for those of us who are divergent thinkers. In fact, it may be the best way to manage our time.

In her book *Time Management for Unmanageable People,* time-management consultant and author Ann McGee-Cooper writes, "If divergent thinkers become blocked on one project, we may shift to another. Frequently, when we are working on the second thing, we understand in a flash what we must do to complete or continue the first project. What seems like a disorganized, misdirected waste of time to the linear convergent person may be a divergent way of keeping the work going while we are waiting for our brain to produce the insights we need."[1] I find this very comforting.

Divergent thinkers can juggle several thoughts at once. While they are weeding the parsley, they may be processing information that will lead to solving a problem with a painting they are working on. Divergent thinkers solve problems by attending to all kinds of things at once and picking out the ideas they need. This ability can make these people seem random and "spacey" to more sequential folks. Furthermore, because divergent thinkers can process many things at once, while they are hoeing around the hollyhocks, they are also paying attention to the sun getting hotter and their backs getting tired. Divergent thinkers know when it's time to do something else for a while. They will get back to their weeding when they need a break from sitting in front of the computer screen or the easel. But when the inspiration they received while weeding the garden has rejuvenated their creative energy, they know it's time to get back to their art.

Convergent thinkers, on the other hand, in their need to experience closure before going on to some other task, will often continue working in the hot sun until they are too tired, sunburned, and sore to do anything creative the rest of the day. Divergent thinkers' apparent randomness can actually be a means of self-preservation.

The point here is that people have many different time-management styles. Just because yours may not be sequential, linear, and assembly-line efficient doesn't make you any less able to use your time wisely. It's all in how you define "using your time wisely." Try this quiz to see what kind of time manager you are.

TIME-MANAGEMENT STYLE QUIZ

Choose the phrase in each statement below that is most true for you.

1. During the course of the day, I usually...
   (a) set goals and accomplish most of them one at a time.
   (b) set goals and achieve only one or two of them, often at the last minute.
   (c) avoid setting goals because it just sets me up for failure.

2. When I have a goal (something I want to do), I...
   (a) go after it with single-minded determination.
   (b) tend to get distracted and start other projects before completing it.
   (c) often get immobilized by anxiety and fail to even get started on it.

3. When I have a deadline (something I have to do within a certain time framework), I usually…

    (a) meet it with time to spare.

    (b) shift into high gear and get it finished just in the nick of time.

    (c) get an extension on the time if possible or, if not, have a good excuse for being late.

4. When I have to be somewhere at a certain time, I…

    (a) usually arrive early or right on time.

    (b) arrive on time or close to it but often have to hurry to make it.

    (c) am almost always late.

5. When I work on a project, I tend to…

    (a) stay focused on it until it is completed.

    (b) become distracted when something else seems more urgent or interesting.

    (c) have so much trouble getting started that sometimes I never begin at all.

6. In my artist studio, office, or workspace, I…

    (a) have a "place for everything and everything in its place."

    (b) have a designated place for things, but I still misplace them.

    (c) am completely random and am never quite sure where I left my tools.

7. I enjoy meetings where…

    (a) the agenda is clearly defined, time is allotted for each item, and the leader sticks to the agenda.

    (b) the agenda is set, but important concerns that arise are allowed to be aired in the course of the meeting.

    (c) the agenda is set by the attendees, not the presenter, and the time allowed reflects the need to resolve each issue before going on to the next.

8. When someone is late for an appointment with me, I…

    (a) get irritated and take it personally.

    (b) only get upset if it makes me late for an opening curtain or the beginning of a program.

    (c) am late myself too often to be irritated by anyone else's tardiness.

9. When it comes to prioritizing tasks, I…

    (a) know pretty well how much time to allot for each one.

    (b) find my priorities change as circumstances change.

    (c) have a hard time prioritizing tasks and don't really adhere to a priority list at all.

10. When I use a day planner or calendar, I…

    (a) block out segments of time needed for each project on my list.

    (b) like to have each major event written down, but don't break down each day into designated segments.

    (c) can never find it when I need it.

If you circled mostly *a*'s in the quiz, you are organized and goal-directed. Congratulations! Your focus may need to be on allowing yourself to participate more freely in "being" behavior that has no real goal or objective. If you are very structured, you may have trouble getting relaxed enough to let the creative ideas flow through you. There is a misconception, however, that all creative people are disorganized and random. I remember quite a few years ago, I walked into a perfectly designed geodesic dome built by Arkansas painter Bob Schub. Schub's art supplies—tools, brushes, palette knives, and tubes of paint—were lined up in rows in a specific place, each lying parallel to the other. Bob, an extremely gifted artist, was not a random kind of guy.

If you are an *a* time manager and you're still not finding time for your daybook, your breathing exercises, and your art, you may be managing to spend much of your time in what I call energy draining rather than energy yielding activities. Use your daybook entries to examine your commitments and ask yourself which ones feed you and which ones deplete you. If you carefully consider the commitments in your life that are more energy draining than energy yielding, you may find that there are at least a few things you can cut from your life that are simply not necessary to your success as a person and an artist. Eliminating unnecessary energy drainers will free up more energy for those pursuits that you believe are necessary and give you more time for more important energy-yielding activities, like practicing your art. If you are an *a* artist, time management is not the problem. Something else is getting in the way of your art.

To every thing there is a season, and a time to every purpose under the heaven…for there is a time for every purpose and for every work.

—Ecclesiastes 3:1,17, KJV

If you chose mainly *b*'s, you are in good company with many artists and other creative thinkers: you function comfortably with a certain amount of ambiguity and randomness. You tend to get distracted while doing one thing, and you may begin something else before the first thing is finished. All creative people are not like this, but many are. Although this randomness can open you to the flow of creative ideas, the problem comes from not being able to stay focused on one thing to completion. Whatever seems important at the moment, whether it's a distressed friend calling to talk about a problem or an idea for a poem that comes in the middle of writing an article that is due the next day, that's what you attend to. *B's* may need to work on setting a specific schedule for their art and sticking to it.

Those who circled mainly *c's*, or a combination of *b's* and *c's*, need a great deal more structure in their lives in order to become more productive artists. Just getting started can seem almost impossible. If you are a *c,* you may have all but given up on believing you are capable of managing your time well. You may even be afraid of what will happen if you do find the time to be more artistic. Using some of the exercises in this chapter and reminding yourself to stop and ask God for help whenever you begin to feel overwhelmed by your lack of time-management skills will help you learn to make time rather than waste time.

TIME MANAGEMENT RESOLUTIONS

Whether you feel inspired to create or dry and uninspired, *you must make time to practice your art.* Here are four resolutions you might find helpful. Some of these will be easier for *a* artists, and others will be easier for *b* or *c* artists. Think of them as healthy time-management guidelines, not commandments or rules.

- I will set aside a specific time for my art every day (if possible).
- I will remind myself that productive artists have schedules and adhere to them.
- I will "go to the studio and make stuff" even when I am dry, frustrated, and clueless as to what to do or where to begin.

- I will not feel guilty about taking time to replenish my sensory reservoir. I will consciously practice breathing in God's inspiration and breathing out the expression of the artistic abilities he has given me.

All four habits are essential for people who want to use time wisely and make time for their art. Notice that making time to create and taking time to just *be* are both a part of this equation. In order to blossom and grow as artists, we have to learn to keep our appointments with the studio as well as with ourselves, and that means doing our breathing exercises—taking ourselves out in order to take in new ideas and sense impressions.

WHAT REALLY MATTERS

You might be surprised to realize how much of your time goes to unnecessary and unimportant activities. There is a popular saying that goes something like this: "Nobody on his deathbed ever said, 'I just wish I'd spent more time at the office.'" To that statement I would add "doing the dishes, maintaining the yard, listening to complaining friends, and sitting in on pointless meetings concerning things I don't really care about." It's not that we don't have time for our art. It's just that we sometimes make unwise choices about how we spend the time we do have.

Time-management experts recommend keeping a record of how we spend our time so that we can get a baseline reading as to where it goes. This is a good exercise even if you only do it for one day. If you can do it for a week, you'll really be able to answer the question, "Who knows where the time goes?" Marshall Cook, in his book *Freeing Your Creativity,* advises:

> Make a place and schedule a time for your artistic activity every day.
> Pay attention to your own biological highs and lows. Work on your
> art when you're the most energetic. Whenever you schedule your

artist time, treat the appointment with your art as you would a date with a cherished friend or treat it as though you are clocking into a job. (You would never skip going to work just because you weren't in the mood!)[2]

EXERCISE 2: TIME CAPSULE

In your daybook or in the space below, keep a record throughout the day of how you spend your time. You might set your watch to beep every hour on the hour. Whenever possible, stop and jot down what you are doing at that moment.

	Activity	**Duration**
Morning	_____	_____
	_____	
	_____	
	_____	
	_____	
	_____	
	_____	
	_____	
Afternoon	_____	_____
	_____	
	_____	
	_____	
	_____	
	_____	
	_____	

TOO MANY IRONS IN THE FIRE

The term *multitasking* has become a part of the language of the workplace. Originally coined to refer to a computer's ability to perform more than one

	Activity	**Duration**
Evening		

Which hat do you wear most of the time: the breadwinner, the caregiver, the household manager, the employee, the boss, the friend, the counselor, the caretaker, the spouse, the parent, or the artist? _____. Is this use of your time working for you, or are you resenting some of the time you spend "doing" for others or doing things you don't feel are really that important?

_____

_____

_____

How does it feel when you manage to salvage an hour or two a day for yourself and your art? Do you ever feel guilty? If so, why? Write about your feelings in your daybook.

calculation or task at a time, it has come to mean the expectation that employees have at least two jobs or projects going on at once. Now people whose styles are more sequential and completion-oriented can actually be perceived as being less productive than those who can juggle multiple tasks simultaneously, even though their productivity might be comparable.

Some would argue that the person who works one task through to completion is the one who is more productive and whose work is less likely to contain errors. Yet the glorification of multitasking has spilled over beyond the work place into many other areas of our lives. If we aren't making appointments on the cell phone while we drive the kids to soccer practice where we drop them off so we can run to the supermarket before we pick them up, only to hurry home to cook dinner while we are helping them with their homework, we feel as though we are being poor parents and providers. Completing one job before going on to the next is no longer an admirable skill.

For many people, sitting in the stands just watching their kids at ball practice makes them antsy as they think about how much they could be accomplishing during that time. It isn't only parents who feel compelled to be doing something (or two or three things) every waking moment of the day. I know single people who get almost panicky when they have an evening that isn't booked with some kind of social, educational, or work-related activity. Their idea of taking time for themselves is to sign up for a personal development workshop during their time off. If they aren't filling their time with semistructured productivity, they feel guilty. I see moms and dads out riding bikes with their kids every evening— while they're talking on cell phones!

We have become a culture of hyperactive adults. In this frenetic society, it is easy to base our sense of self-worth on how many activities we can handle at one time rather than on how well we are doing each task, how much we are enjoying it, or how much time we're willing to set aside and protect in order to do the things that really matter to us.

When did we switch from living by our mother's advice to "slow down, honey, and just do one thing at a time" to living like jugglers who have four plates and a chair in the air all day long? It is no wonder so many of us suffer from stress, anxiety, and depression. If we're not behaving as though we're super-human, we don't feel worthy. Maybe we just need to learn to say yes to saying no.

Saying Yes to Saying No

Ask yourself how much time you spend each week doing what other people want you to do instead of doing what you really wish you could be doing. Do you ever feel so overcommitted to activities, responsibilities, and social events that you end up feeling resentful rather than enjoying the rewards of service to others? Do you take on things you'd rather not do just so you will look good to other people? Do you ever feel pressured into taking on additional commitments even though you wish you could reply, like Nathaniel Hawthorne's Bartleby the Scrivener, "I'd prefer not to"?

> *To get all there is out of living, we must employ our time wisely, never being in too much of a hurry to stop and sip life, but never losing our sense of the enormous value of a minute.*
>
> —ROBERT UPDEGRAFF

When we say yes to someone else's needs or desires, we are often saying no to our own. In fact, any time we make a decision about how to spend our time and energy, we are saying no to something. In order to protect and honor the time we've set aside to be artists, we must find the courage to say no to the appropriate things.

Giving our time, our resources, and our talents to help others is a good thing. We are, the Bible tells us, the light of the world, the salt of the earth. As we've discussed, we need to move past self-absorption and self-centeredness in order to become servants to the work God has given us. Saying no to others may seem like a move back toward focus on the self. Doesn't "dying to self" mean becoming a willing servant to others? Isn't saying no just another kind of preoccupation with self? No. (See how easy that was?)

Saying no is not always negative. Saying no can be proactive and positive. Anne Morrow Lindbergh, in *Gift from the Sea,* writes, "There are so few empty pages in my engagement pad or empty hours in the day or empty rooms in my life in which to stand alone and find myself.... Too many worthy activities, valuable things, and interesting people. For it is not merely the trivial which clutters our lives but the important as well. We can have a surfeit of treasures—an excess of shells, where one or two would be significant."[3] We, too, can have a surfeit of good things in our lives. The people we care about are important to us, and we want to spend time nurturing those relationships. But some of us base our sense of self-worth on how well we respond to the needs of others. Saying no might seem rude or selfish. With practice, however, we will stop feeling guilty and begin to sense a kind of respect from the very people whose requests we have learned to decline. I know from personal experience that people actually admire me for taking a stand that they wish they had the courage to take. This surprising reaction to protecting time for art will reinforce the healthy habit of saying no.

Think about the things in your life you would most like to be able to say no to. Having dinner with your in-laws? Going to the monthly PTA officers' meetings? Staying in the bell choir? Going out with that friend who drains your energy and is no fun for you to be with? Watching television with your spouse when you'd rather be doing something creative? Going to work? Cleaning the house? List below three things to which you wish you could just say no. (No matter how impossible it may seem to ever learn to say no to these things, write them down anyway.)

_____

_____

_____

Whenever you need to decide whether you are within the bounds of courtesy and kindness to refuse a request for your time, ask yourself, "If I were at a job in the working world right now instead of trying to protect my artist time at home, would I be asked to do this?" If the answer is no, then you should say no to that person's request. Your artist time is as important as working-outside-the-home time.

This test is also useful when you are feeling as though you should be spending your time doing something other than working with your art (like mopping the kitchen floor or washing the car). Ask yourself, "Would I be doing this chore if I were at work right now instead of at home? What awful thing will happen if I just hit the kitchen floor with the electric broom and waited a week or so to mop it?" By worst-casing the consequences of saying no to certain items on your to-do list, you will see that what you thought needed to be done can easily go undone a little while longer. And all those little whiles add up to more time for your art.

Avoiding the "I'm Indispensable" Trap

Another roadblock to saying no is the belief that you are indispensable. *The play can't go on unless I am the music director. The club will fold if I don't agree to be president. My friend will go into a deep depression if I don't meet her for lunch.* What's wrong with this way of thinking?

To begin with, the conviction that our participation is vital to the success of an enterprise is self-centered. Do we really believe the project can't be completed without us? We all know people who come to work when they are sick because they think they are indispensable. The truth is, their devotion to their job can cause them to stay sick longer, infect other people, and become a hindrance to whatever work they think can't be done without them. Behaving as though you believe the world will collapse without your participation is a delusion, and you need to get over it for the sake of your own mental and artistic health.

The "I'm indispensable" trap can be harmful in other ways. Is there anyone in your life who calls and talks to you for long periods of time, who pursues you for lunch or coffee dates not because you have a deep, abiding friendship, but because they want to process their problems with you? It may even be somewhat flattering to have your opinion and advice sought after. But unless you are trained in the field of psychotherapy, the time you give these people that may not be particularly helpful because it can get in the way of their getting the help they really need. The illusion that you are indispensable to their well-being can actually be harmful to them as well as a hindrance to your efforts at making more time for yourself as an artist.

There is a difference between nurturing true friendships and allowing ourselves to be used as sounding boards by people who are emotionally needy and require more help than we can give them. The way to avoid these time sinks is to tell your needy acquaintance that you aren't booking any dates until your current project is completed. Another way to put it is "I'm sorry, but I'm already over-committed and I just can't put another thing on my calendar right now." Don't allow yourself to be coerced into spending time with people who drain your

---

EXERCISE 3: HOW DO I REFUSE THEE? LET ME COUNT THE WAYS...

Think of some ways you can politely say no to other people's requests for your time. Write at least three of them on the lines below.

_____

_____

_____

_____

_____

_____

energy and steal your time. If you don't particularly look forward to spending time with the needy people in your life, chances are they are not true friends anyway.

Once you start taking care of yourself and stop thinking that other people can't function without you, you'll be surprised by how supportive some of those people can be. They will admire your efforts to take care of yourself and to protect your time. You will be using that time to be alone with God, to open up to his inspiration, to feel yourself come alive and know a new sense of wholeness. This "new and improved" you will be a blessing to the people around you.

The truth is—listen carefully to this one—other people really *can* get along without you! The world will go on if the laundry doesn't get done. No matter what the chairperson tells you, the bake sale will succeed without your famous caramel pecan brownies. The fundraiser will proceed even if you are too busy writing your book to sell magazine subscriptions at work for your kids. The investment club will survive even if you don't agree to be the treasurer. The family will not starve if you don't cook for them every night. Instead of saying, "I'd love to practice my art, but I just don't have the time," try saying, "I'd love to help you out with _____, but I just don't have the time. I need to go practice my art."

Time is the coin of your life. It is the only coin you have, and only you can determine how it will be spent. Be careful lest you let other people spend it for you.

—CARL SANDBURG

Serving our gift is not *self*-serving; it is *God*-serving. As we become servants to our talents, we become more fulfilled. We stop trying to please others at the expense of nurturing the artist within us. We become happier, more at peace, less resentful, and more fun to be around. Saying no to other people is saying yes to God's desire for us to develop the gifts he gave us.

TAKING BACK YOUR LIFE

One New Year's Eve about two years ago, I resolved to take "the year of saying no" so I could finally act on my dream of becoming a writer. I stopped doing the music at my church once a month, quit giving piano lessons, declined all offers to work on committees, didn't run for office in the club I'd presided over for two years, and decided not to volunteer for anything extra. I also learned to be more selective in accepting invitations for social engagements. Simply put, I pulled inward and began the work of clearing my daily calendar to find more time to write.

At first I worried that people would think me a self-centered slacker. When people asked me to volunteer for something, I'd say, "I'm sorry, but I'm having 'the year of saying no.' I'm not taking on anything extra for a year just to see if I can get better control of my life." What do you think happened? Did everyone I know think I was selfish, no longer a team player, or just out of my mind? Did people get angry with me? Did I lose all my friends?

I was delightfully surprised to find that not only did most people not get angry or seem annoyed when I told them, but they almost always said something like, "What a lovely idea! I need a 'year of saying no,' too. I just can't seem to refuse when people ask me to do something. I always feel guilty and end up saying yes."

My year of saying no was so successful that many people who know me got out of the habit of asking me to do things, so I now have fewer people to turn down. Not only did I have a wonderful and relatively stress-free year, but I also learned that my world—including work, family, friends, chores, clubs, and church—all got on perfectly well without me. My family was supportive of my resolution, especially after they got used to the more relaxed person who was much easier to live with than the one who had been so overextended before. Also, by declaring my year of saying no, I gave others permission to do the same.

And that's what I'm giving you now—permission to do the same. (You knew this was coming, didn't you?) If a year seems too long, try saying no for three months. However much or little you commit to, go easy on yourself. If you say no to a request so that you can stay home and paint and then do nothing but read and take a nap, that's okay. Don't jump off one treadmill onto another, or you will lose the joy and wonder of what you are trying to do. Your body, mind, and spirit know what you need to be healthy. You are giving yourself the gift of time; that is what matters.

In your daybook write about whether you think you can give yourself this gift. Tell your family about your decision. Assure them that this does not mean you will quit doing the things that need to be done, but let them know that there will be times when they want you to do things for them, and you will say no to them. Ask for their support. The added peace and quiet, plus the new you, might make life easier for everyone around the house.

Practice using the "decliners" you came up with in Exercise 3. Don't hedge by saying, "I'm having the year of saying no, but I'll be happy to take over as PTA president next year." That will only put you under the burden of a future commitment that you may not be able to (or want to) keep when the time comes. Besides, the onus of that impending responsibility might tarnish the gloss of your year off. It's okay to say no without explanation and without making promises about "next time" or "later."

When you need to say yes to a special event, set specific parameters ("I can see you from 11:30 to 1:00 on Thursday") and then stick to the time frame you've set. Believe that it is healthy for you to set limits and to protect yourself from being pressured into allowing those boundaries to be breached. Pray for God to strengthen you in your resolve to protect your artist time. As you practice your year of saying no, record the changes it makes in how you feel as an artist and how you feel about your life in general. Rejoice in your improved mental and spiritual health!

Fasting from the Telephone

Another way to buy more time to be an artist is to quit answering your phone. Let your voice mail or answering service take your calls, and then return them all at once when you're on a break. This sounds like a simple thing, yet I have many friends and family members who simply cannot resist the temptation to answer when they hear the rings, even if they are busy with other things. My sister, for example, has both a gift for encouraging others and a very hard time not answering her telephone. She worries that the caller might be someone who needs to talk over problems with her. Unfortunately, this answered call may mean spending an hour of her best artist-energy time talking on the phone.

If what they have to say is important enough, callers will leave a message, and you can get back to them on your free time. I have recently switched from an answering machine to the answering service offered by my local phone company. Not only do I not miss any incoming calls when I'm online or on the phone, but I don't even have to hear the voice of the person calling. When I do give in and pick up before the answering service does, it usually turns out to be an unwelcome call from a solicitor or some other intrusive space invader. (Or maybe it was someone who would have preferred to leave a quick message on my answering service anyway.) The time it takes me to walk to the phone, answer it, and then get rid of the caller (politely, of course) is time I could have spent writing or practicing. If I answer and the person on the other end is someone I care about, I'm liable to say, "I can talk only a minute," and that minute turns into half an hour. In any case, just trying to get my concentration back takes away from artist time. How many times per day do you say to yourself, "Let's see, where was I?"

When you're tempted to answer your phone, ask yourself, "What would happen if this call came while I wasn't home?" Even at work, most of us have disciplined ourselves not to take personal calls while we're on the clock. As a teacher with a phone in her classroom, I can tell you that if I answered while I'm supposed to be teaching, the taxpayer on the other end of the line (who pays my salary) wouldn't be happy about it. Most people expect to leave voice-mail messages these days and are happy to do so. The simple practice of letting your answering machine or answering service take your calls, and then returning them when you are on your break, can buy you as much as an hour of artist time a day.

EXERCISE 4: TELEPHONE LIBERATION

For practice, don't answer your phone this week whether or not you are on the artist-time clock. Let your answering machine take messages for you.

If you do give in and pick up the telephone, write down the following information in this log. (You need not count calls you are returning or making on your own.) At the end of the week, add up the time you spent on the phone—that could've been artist time!

Caller's Name	Date	Time Spent Talking

Like writing down what you eat when you are on a diet, tracking the time you spend on the phone will help you see how much time you are consuming by picking it up every time it rings. Sometimes just knowing you're going to have to take the trouble to log the conversation will keep you from reaching for that receiver.

One more tip for those of you who are parents or caretakers of your own parents, those of you who find yourself at a time of your life when someone counts on being able to get in touch with you whenever they need you. Have a signal you use with only those people and make sure they know to use the signal only if their call is pretty important. You might, for instance, have them let the phone ring twice and then hang up. Then they should call back, and you'll answer it if you're home because you'll know who is calling. I use this system and it works very well.

When you allow your time to be held hostage by the needs of others (in this case, someone else's need to talk to you at a time that may not be convenient for you), you lose control of your time. You are exercising neither self-control nor control of your time when you pick up the phone every time it rings. You can be a good friend, a faithful parent and spouse, and a reliable colleague, even if you let your answering machine or voice mail answer the phone for you. All you have to do is return your calls when you are on a break from working on your art. Try it. I think you'll like it.

Reining in the E-mail Monster

A chapter on time management wouldn't be complete without addressing one of the latest time-consumers in many people's lives: reading and responding to e-mail. Whenever we talk about fasting from the phone in the *Creative Call* groups I lead, someone mentions how much time they spend keeping up with their e-mail. Here are a few suggestions for maintaining control over this electronic distraction.

- Just as you are doing with the phone, set specific times for answering e-mail. If you have a "You've Got Mail" type of indicator and you work a lot on your computer, as many writers and graphic artists do, just turn off the You've Got Mail signal. Most e-mail messages aren't so urgent that they need an immediate answer.

- Check your e-mail on your schedule, not on somebody else's schedule.

- Remember that the beauty of the e-mail system is that someone can e-mail you when it's convenient for them, and you can answer when it's convenient for you. If you check your e-mail every time you hear that *beep,* you are eliminating one of the main advantages e-mail has over phone calls: having control over when you devote your time to it.

Turning Off Your TV

When I was in high school in the late sixties, each day in our home began with *The Today Show* and ended with *The Tonight Show.* The television would often be left on even when no one was watching it. The programs droning on in the background may have changed (and not necessarily for the better), but in most American homes this scenario has not.

According to a 1998 study conducted by the A. C. Nielsen Company, a television is on in the average American home 7 hours, 12 minutes each day. Americans watch 3 hours and 46 minutes of TV daily, more than 52 days of nonstop TV watching per year. By age sixty-five most Americans will have spent nearly 9 years sitting through mostly mindless programming or channel surfing from one forgettable offering to another, one year of which will have been spent watching commercials. And what is happening to the outdated concept of the family conversing around the dinner table when 66 percent of Americans regularly watch television while eating dinner?

My husband, son, and I gave up watching television completely when my son was fourteen. It took James about two weeks to get over missing it; within six months he was telling people that not only did he not miss it, but he actually felt better off for not having it in his life. (He thought it was cool to say that he lived in a TV-free house.) Dinner times turned into leisurely opportunities to discuss our days and talk about ideas. (You'd be amazed how many thoughts teenagers are willing to express when they know they have an attentive audience.) Both my husband and I found more time to pay attention to our art: he to practice lines for whatever plays he is in or to learn new music for one of his singing groups, and I to practice either writing, the piano, or the hammered dulcimer I own but have never learned to play.

Whether or not you have children in the home, I urge you to consider unplugging your television. I realize this won't be easy, but it's a surefire way of getting serious about finding time for your art. You can keep current with world events by reading newspapers and other periodicals and by listening to National Public Radio while you're doing other things. You can entertain yourself by taking walks, playing games, reading, having conversations with the people you love, playing with your art, and doing some of the breathing exercises mentioned earlier in the book.

 I find television very educational. Every time someone switches it on,
I go into another room and read a good book.

—GROUCHO MARX

If you find yourself using television as a way to unwind, if you come away from TV viewing feeling worse than when you sat down to watch it, if you regularly fall asleep in front of the TV, if in the morning you have trouble even remembering what you watched the night before, try the next exercise. Think of it as rearranging the furniture.

EXERCISE 5: FINDING A NEW PLACE FOR THE TV

- Move your television set into a closet or other storage area for one month. If your set is too big to move, cover it with something interesting and make it an "art piece." (Slap one of those collages or posters you've made in the past weeks onto the front of it!) Unplug it, hide the remote control, and don't turn it on, ever, for a whole month.

- Make it as difficult as you can to give in to the temptation to watch TV. Don't read the TV guide section of the paper, for example, or engage in conversations at work with people who are discussing last night's shows. Plan specific activities— going for walks, taking family time, or working in the studio—for the time you normally spend in front of the tube.

- Don't wait until after "the sweeps" (there will always be "specials"), or until after the holidays (there are always holidays), or until after a particular sports season is over (it's always sports season). If there is a program or sporting event that you really want to see, go to a friend's house or to a local sports bar and make watching that show a social occasion. Eliminate television as a part of your everyday life for one month. Keep a record of your successes and your lapses.

- Don't think of yourself as a loser if you give in. It takes a month to break a habit or forge a new one. Use this experiment as a subject for your daybook writing. Don't forget to pray for the strength to reach your TV-free goal.

What do you think? Will you go through TV withdrawal? Will you not know what to do with yourself in the evening? Will you read, write, paint, putter, play cards with your family, exercise more, go out more? Will you make gifts instead of spending time and money buying them? Will you cook dinners, sew, build something, write letters? Will you go to bed earlier? Will you feel better about others because you're not internalizing all the negative messages coming through the airwaves? Won't it be interesting to find out?

WHAT'S THE PAYOFF?

Does all this sound too radical? Do you feel as though you are being asked to change who you are, to quit being the helpful person you pride yourself on being, to fast from the technology you rely on? If so, then let's remind ourselves of the reason for our trying to make time for our art: not because we ought to, but because unless we do, we will never wholly become the people God created us to be.

In addressing the question of time, Charles E. Hummel wrote, "Our dilemma goes deeper than shortage of time; it is basically a problem of priorities. We confess, 'We have left undone those things that we ought to have done; and we have done those things which we ought not to have done.'"[4] We have the Holy Spirit within us to help us with our priorities, the Spirit of light who waits to be called upon so he can help us make the time we need to be the artists God calls us to be.

When we find the time to engage in our art, we engage in a kind of ministry. Madeleine L'Engle says that artists "draw people to Christ by…showing them a light that is so lovely that they want with all their hearts to know the source of it. If our lives are truly 'hid with Christ in God,' the astounding thing is that this hiddenness is revealed in all that we do and say and write."[5] Making time for the Spirit of God to work through the talents he has given us is creating a kind of prayer time. In those minutes or hours, we give back to God some of what he has given us: attention, time, and talent. We offer him the new spaces we create in our lives so that he can speak to us, inspire us, and answer our prayer that we learn how to follow his creative call. Making time means allowing ourselves to attend to our artist work in hopes that we will give something special back to the world, something that might reveal that "light that is so lovely that [others] will want with all their hearts to know the source of it." "Greater is he who is in you than he who is in the world" (I John 4:4, NASB). This is the promise and the hope.

And hope does not disappoint,
because the love of God has been
poured out within our hearts through
the Holy Spirit who was given to us.
—ROMANS 5:5, NASB

CHAPTER EIGHT

SIMPLIFYING

Be anxious for nothing, but in everything by prayer and supplication
with thanksgiving let your requests be made known to God.
And the peace of God, which surpasses all comprehension,
shall guard your hearts and your minds in Christ Jesus.

PHILIPPIANS 4:6-7, NASB

*I*n 1973 I left Florida and moved to northwest Arkansas with my first husband and four other friends. More than anything, we wanted the freedom
and space to live more creatively, to build our own houses, grow our own food,
and make our own clothing and furniture. Although none of us were professional
artists, among us were a painter, a sculptor, a graphic artist, two writers, and a
musician: quite the band of gypsies. We bought 120 mountainous acres, sold
almost everything we owned, and headed out with youthful enthusiasm to "live
off the fat of the land" in the rugged Ozark Mountains. We naively believed that
by not working outside the home, by raising our own food, and by building our
own houses instead of being burdened by mortgage debt, we would be free to
develop ourselves as artists and live a healthier, more natural lifestyle.

After several months valiantly attempting to clear the land with hand tools,
we pooled the little money we had left and hired a bulldozer operator to cut a
road and a clearing into the woods so we could plant an orchard and build a small

cabin. Then we realized we needed money for a well if we were to live in that clearing and keep the fruit trees and garden alive. We fought ticks and chiggers in the summer and icy, mud-slick dirt roads in the winter. Once we ran out of money and had to get regular jobs to support ourselves, we also had to move in closer to "the blacktop." In addition to all the work we'd taken on in order to live a "simpler" life, we now found ourselves back on the workaday treadmill, trying to both pay our modest bills and earn enough money to continue our back-to-the-land project. And this was all so we could have more time for our art!

> *Our life is frittered away by detail.... Simplify, simplify.*
>
> —HENRY DAVID THOREAU

Even after the other four people moved back to the city, my husband and I stayed and built a house with our own hands on twenty-five acres that were not quite so remote. In taking on this project I was fulfilling a dream I had nurtured since I read *Swiss Family Robinson* at the age of ten. Answering that need to be more creative had brought me to Mountainburg to begin with. We cut our own firewood and pumped our water from a wet-weather spring that dried up to a trickle every summer. We fought drought, insects, deer, and groundhogs for our share of the fruit and vegetables we tried to raise in our half-acre organic garden. I learned to hang and finish plasterboard, to lay hardwood flooring, and to do plumbing, roofing, and electrical work. For the first eleven years we lived without air conditioning, even though it stopped raining from July through mid-September and temperatures at or near one hundred degrees for several days running were not uncommon. Keeping cool meant dips in the few spring-fed "swimming holes" that still held water in spite of the drought. In an attempt to cool the house (without the expense of air conditioning), my husband installed a huge attic fan that sucked in enough hot air to turn the inside of our house into one huge convection oven. Many years I would teach summer school at a community college an hour's drive away, as much to be in the air conditioning as to earn the extra money.

The first year we were in Arkansas, we lived in a house that had no indoor plumbing. The entire thirteen winters we were there, we heated our various houses with a wood-burning stove. When sudden ice storms hit the mountaintop, we would come home from our teaching jobs in the valley to an ice-glazed wood-pile and a freezing cold house on top of Cartwright Mountain. If we had neglected to bring in dry wood before we left home that morning, we would have to beat the woodpile with axes or sledgehammers to dislodge some of the smaller sleet-encrusted logs. If we were lucky, we might coax the stove's few remaining coals into a fire hot enough to ignite the waterlogged firewood by feeding those embers newspapers and wood chips from the basement workshop. After working up sufficient body heat to quit caring about a roaring fire, we would finally succeed in bringing enough wood into the house to make it through the night without the water pipes freezing and bursting. It didn't take many of these experiences before we learned to keep a good supply of dry wood in the basement.

I moved back to Winter Park, Florida, in 1986. During the first cold snap of what passes for winter here, I walked across the living room to the thermostat on the wall and turned on the furnace with one small movement of my index finger. "This," I said to my son James, "is simplifying our lifestyle!"

WHAT DOES IT MEAN TO SIMPLIFY?

I tell this story to make the point that when I use the word *simplifying*, I do not mean a back-to-nature, Mother Earth philosophy of disconnecting from the system. I've done that, and, as the story above illustrates, there is nothing simple about it. Self-sufficiency and simplifying one's life are not synonymous. Having your own pressure cleaner or gas-powered generator might make you more self-reliant, but having to pay for, maintain, and store another piece of machinery will not make your life less complicated. Turning your backyard into a vegetable garden will help you be less dependent on the grocery store, but unless you love gardening for its own sake, it will neither simplify your life nor give you more time to spend on your art.

If we want to hear God's voice and his calling for us as artists, and if we want to live a life that is conducive to answering that call, we need to simplify our lives—in the true sense of the word *simplify*. Living a simple life is a very old ideal. Great thinkers and writers since the dawn of recorded time have counseled people to live simply. The ancient Greek philosopher Democritus (460-370 B.C.) wrote, "Let your occupations be few if you would lead a tranquil life." Roman Emperor Marcus Aurelius Antoninus (A.D. 121-180) agreed with Democritus that we should reduce the number of things we do in our lives, and he also warned us about complicating our lives with too many *things*. He wrote: "Let not your mind run on what you lack as much as on what you have already" and "Remember this—that very little is needed to make a happy life."

Jesus taught that, in order to have an authentic relationship with our Creator, we must trust God and not get caught up in the worries and busyness of life. In Luke 12, Jesus instructs, "Therefore I tell you, do not worry about your life, what you will eat; or about your body, what you will wear" (verse 22). Then he asks his listeners to consider the lilies of the field, how God arrays them in simple beauty. Jesus also speaks of simplifying our lives so we can know God better in Mark 10:17 and 21. When the rich young man asks, "Good teacher, what must I do to inherit eternal life?," Jesus answers, much to the young man's chagrin and discomfiture, "Go, sell everything you have and give to the poor, and you will have treasure in heaven. Then come, follow me." In other words, we are to give up our attachment to the things of this world and then follow the calling God is offering us.

Henry David Thoreau and Ralph Waldo Emerson were but two of the literary and philosophical voices speaking for simplicity in the nineteenth century. The twentieth century had its share of advocates for simplifying life, as the story of my personal back-to-the-land pilgrimage illustrates. Currently, books and magazines teem with information on how to live more simply, and there are Web sites and consultants dedicated to only one thing: teaching people how to simplify their lives. That fact alone tells us that we still don't get it. In her article "Simplifying Life," Susan Pilgrim writes, "Not since the days of Thoreau has there been such an emphasis on simplifying life. As a generation, the Baby Boomers have had it all—cars, status, big homes, money, and lots of stress. They're discovering that 'having it all' isn't everything it's cracked up to be. Something has been missing. That something is meaning. Fundamentally, 'simplifying' is determining what's really important to you."[1]

Artists know their art is important to them, so a major motivator for simplifying life can be to make more time to be artists. We need to step off the materialism treadmill and start trusting God to meet our needs. In this chapter we will explore ways to make life less complicated, less busy, and less stressful so that we can live more creatively. We will look at how to make conscious choices based on what is really important to us as well as to declutter our life, get control of finances, and step out of fear into faith.

EXERCISE 1: WHAT MATTERS TO ME

Make a list of the top ten things that are important in your life. This list doesn't have to be in any particular order of importance. Just write down ten things that really matter to you. Afterwards, you may go back and prioritize them.

_____

_____

_____

_____

_____

_____

_____

_____

_____

_____

Look over the list you just made. Does any pattern emerge? What really matters to you? Is it family, friends, and relationships in general? Are career goals high on your list? Your relationship with God? Did you mention developing your artistic talents? Do you have a desire to travel or to study? How much of what is important to you is related to money or the lack of money? If you discovered that you had only six months left to live, which of the things on your list would suddenly rise to the top? If you had to pare the list down to only five things, what would they be? Now ask yourself whether you are willing to let some of the less important things go in order to simplify your life and have more time for the things you want to keep.

Deciding what is important is the first step in simplifying our lives. If being with friends and family is high on the list, then we need to evaluate whether or not the life we are currently living reflects that value. What choices are we making in our daily lives that keep us from devoting time to what is important?

If you dedicate some time to praying, thinking, and writing about what really matters to you, you will be taking a giant step toward simplifying your life. More

---

EXERCISE 2: THINKING ABOUT WHAT MATTERS

This week as you write in your daybook, you may wish to take one or two items from the list you made in Exercise 1 and address the following:

1. Why is this important to me?

2. Am I spending the kind of time and energy I'd like focusing on this? If not, why not? What is getting in the way?

3. What in my life or my schedule would I be willing to change or give up in order to start paying more attention to this significant aspect of my life?

than half of changing what isn't working for you is *recognizing* what isn't working. I encourage you to spend some time with Exercise 2 this week so that you can get the pieces of your life laid out before you and start moving them around for a better fit. Once you have clearly defined what is important, you can start using those items as standards for choosing how you want to spend your life.

THE FOREST FOR THE TREES

It can be hard to identify what matters to us because these days we have so many choices. We are overloaded with options, temptations, stimuli, and obligations. We have to plow through so much stuff, so many commitments, so many decisions, that we become exhausted before we've even begun. With so much pressing in on us, it's hard to see clearly how to start simplifying our lives.

In forestry there are two main methods for removing timber: clear cutting, where everything goes down to the bulldozer and chain saw, and selective logging, in which only the trees deemed past their prime are taken out. The latter is much like what we do when we start thinning out the things in our lives that take our time and energy without giving either back to us. We need to selectively prune away the things in our lives that are not life-giving, thereby allowing more space for the important things, more space for the "healthy trees" to grow.

My friend Dave, who works in public relations, is a talented musician. A single guy with a modest income, he believed he needed to have a roommate to afford a decent place to live. Even though a roommate eased his financial burdens somewhat, Dave always felt uncomfortable practicing his saxophone at home because he worried he was disturbing his roommate. Once the band he plays in started getting regular paid gigs, Dave made the decision to move to a place of his own. By choosing to put his music before his worry about finances, he has been able to practice whenever he wants, guilt-free, and is now working steadily as a musician. He hasn't quit his day job yet, but the extra money he gets from being in his band is helping to offset the financial strain of no longer having a roommate. By thinning out one area of his life, he was able to make a clearing for what is really important to him.

Whoever Has the Most Toys Loses

One way to thin out the forest of our life is to go through all our possessions and decide what we can do without. "Getting rid of the clutter is not about letting go of the things that are meaningful to you. It's about letting go of the things that no longer contribute to your life so you have the time and the energy and the space for the things that do," writes Elaine St. James in *Living the Simple Life*.[2] Deciding what to keep and what not to can be a daunting task, but it must be done if you want to escape the bondage that possessions can keep you in.

Steven Catlin, author of *Work Less and Play More*, refers to what he calls the Law of Possessions: "Each and every possession extracts a toll in time and money." He gives the following advice about getting rid of our superfluous belongings: "Look at all possessions with a critical eye. Ask yourself, 'Is this something that I either (1) need, or (2) enjoy on a regular basis?' If you can't honestly say 'yes' on either count, place the item on the 'condemned' pile.... Don't ask yourself, 'Will I use this in the next year?' Instead ask, 'Have I used this in the past year?'"[3]

My friend Nancy often puts things she's not sure she's ready to part with in a box that she leaves in her garage for a year. Anything she hasn't retrieved from the box after a year goes to charity when the grace period is over. How do you deal with eliminating possessions in your life? Write down your approach in your daybook.

We all own special items we may want to keep for sentimental reasons even if we don't "need or enjoy them on a regular basis." A twenty-five-year collection of journals, the boxes of photographs I hope I'll someday take the time to organize into albums, CDs I only listen to during the holiday season, my collection of sheet music, and my grandmother's china are examples of possessions I want to keep even though they are not used regularly. For every one of those, however, there are probably ten items that I don't need cluttering up my closets, shelves, and drawers. Be careful not to give in to excessive sentimental attachment to possessions. Be judicious in choosing what is worth keeping. Attachment to our possessions is not conducive to simplifying, nor is it biblical. The Bible admonishes us to put our trust and our faith in God and not in money or possessions. In Matthew 6:19-21, Jesus warns us, "Do not store up for yourselves treasures on earth, where moth and rust destroy, and where thieves break in and steal. But store up for yourselves treasures in heaven.... For where your treasure is, there your heart will be also."

In *Walden* Henry David Thoreau proposes that "a man is rich in proportion to the number of things which he can afford to let alone." What he means is the fewer possessions a person feels he or she needs to have, the richer that person's life is. How much of what we own or what we want to own could we really "afford to let alone," afford to do without? In what ways does the elimination of possessions simplify our lives?

EXERCISE 3: THINGS I CAN DO WITHOUT

Take a walk through your house and write down everything you could do without. Use the lines below or make this your daybook entry for today.

_____

_____

_____

_____

_____

_____

_____

When you are ready, take your list of things you can do without and gather up the items you wrote down. Have a garage sale or call your favorite charity to come pick up these items. If you aren't ready yet, save your list until you are ready, or put those things in the garage or a storage area for their year of grace before you sell or give them away. The knowledge that you cannot see the beauty of your own private "forest" for all the superfluous "trees" you have been holding on to may be enough to help you eliminate some of the things that clutter and complicate your life.

Simple Honesty

This section of the chapter doesn't apply to everyone, and if you are a scrupulously honest person, you may choose to skip it altogether. Most of us, however, find ourselves from time to time in situations where it just seems easier and, we reason, *kinder* to tell a lie than to tell the truth. Most of us also know that every time we do this, we complicate our lives. When we step out of the safety of total honesty, we take on the complication of covering up that dishonesty. Once the untruth is told, we have to focus our attention and direct our energy toward making sure we don't slip up and contradict ourselves in later conversations. Few of us can say we have never lived out the old adage, "O, what a tangled web we weave when first we practice to deceive." Absolute commitment to honesty is a practice that simplifies our lives and doesn't cost us a thing.

Proverbs 14:2 tells us, "Those who walk uprightly fear the LORD, but one who is devious in conduct despises him" (NRSV). That statement seems pretty clear. The reason the Lord wants us to be honest also seems clear. When we are dishonest, we demonstrate a lack of faith in him. When we resort to dishonesty, we are, in a sense, "playing God": manipulating the truth to get our needs met rather than trusting God to meet those needs. Dishonesty is a complication that not only keeps us from simplifying our lives, but it also gets in the way of our maintaining a clear and open relationship with God, something we need if we are to breathe in the inspiration of the Holy Spirit. Scrupulous honesty is one way to remove needless complication from our lives while we build a stronger relationship with God and become more attuned to the inspiration of the Holy Spirit.

Search me, O God, and know my heart; test me and know my anxious thoughts.

—PSALMS 139:23

Simplifying our lives is a spiritual issue and an act of faith. So is choosing to live honestly. When we make the commitment to absolute honesty in every aspect of our lives, we eliminate cover-ups, entanglements, second-guessing, and the need to remember to whom we told what. We also demonstrate our faith in God to meet our needs. Commit yourself to complete honesty and make your life less complicated. Practice the art of telling the truth without offering unnecessarily hurtful opinions. Don't make up phony excuses to get out of doing something you don't want to do. Don't call in sick when you're not sick—take a personal day instead, even if you have to take a loss in pay as a result. Trust God to meet your financial needs so that you can resist the temptation to "borrow" supplies from the workplace or inflate deductions on your income tax return. We are complex people who are involved with other complex people in our very complex everyday lives, and that basic reality presents enough entanglements for us to deal with. We don't need to make more of our own. Complete honesty in word and deed eliminates the complication of covering up the dishonesty, thereby simplifying our lives. And remember, the less complicated our lives are, the more time, space, and energy we can devote to our art.

If you are still hanging in with me on this part of the chapter and are willing to take a real challenge, try Exercise 4 in your daybook. Examine your conscience and look at the ways you have not been perfectly honest. Think of how dishonesty, even in small ways, has complicated your life and, without your realizing it, impeded the development of your art.

The point of Exercise 4 is to get honest with ourselves and with God. Even if it is too late or impossible for you to make amends for what you did, your written confession will be good for your spirit, it will be good for the artist in you, and it will help strengthen your commitment to honesty in the future. It will open the channels of communication between you and your muse, the Holy Spirit of God. When we confess our sin, either in prayer or in writing, we clear the air and reopen the lines of communion between His Spirit and us. "God is light; in him there is no darkness at all. If we claim to have fellowship with him yet walk in the darkness, we lie and do not live by the truth.... If we confess our sins, he is faithful and just and will forgive us our sins and purify us from all unrighteousness" (1 John 1:5-6,9). Resolve to get honest about past dishonesties. Accept God's forgiveness. Strive for total honesty in the future. Taking these steps will not only make you feel better about yourself and help declutter your life, it will also open up both your time and your consciousness to working on your art in a more deliberate, Christ-centered way.

EXERCISE 4: "CREATE IN ME A PURE HEART, O GOD..."

Read Psalm 51. Write an entry that begins with the phrase, "Nobody knows about the time I..." and then tell about something dishonest you once did, especially if it resulted in complications in your life. Remember, you don't have to share this with anyone.

THE MONEY QUESTION

One reason some people walk the line between honesty and dishonesty is that they suffer from fear about not having enough money. Making money and worrying about having enough money can sap our creative energy. Fear and anxiety for any reason can kill the creative spirit. Anxiety comes from many sources and in many forms, but at least part of it results from not trusting that God "will never fail you nor forsake you" (Deuteronomy 31:6). Yet ask a group of reawakening artists to name what keeps them from making a total commitment to their art, and most reply, "It's the money. I can't afford to quit my day job, and I don't have any energy when I get home to practice my art." Worry and anxiety about money—not to mention the energy it takes to make the money we think we need to live—can paralyze an artist. Do any of the following statements sound familiar?

- I worry about the initial costs of the materials I need to practice my art.
- I worry about whether the time I spend on art will take away from the time I should spend making money.
- I have to work outside the home to earn a living, but I'm so exhausted at the end of the workday that I don't have the energy to enjoy working on my talents. I am just too tired to be creative.
- The ideal of working less so I can "play around" with my art more seems irresponsible and unrealistic.
- I'm afraid that I'll put all that time into my art, and I won't ever make any money from it.

If you can relate to any of these statements, money issues may be getting in the way of your feeling free to pay attention to practicing your art. This part of the chapter touches on three ideas that will simplify the financial segment of your life and help free you to develop your art: getting out of debt, spending less than you make, and saving for what you need. If you are willing to do your part, God will supply what you need to get your financial house in order so that you can be free to be the artist he desires you to be.

Cast all your anxiety on him because he cares for you.

—1 PETER 5:7

One way to alleviate anxiety over money concerns is to get out and stay out of debt. Monthly payments add to the burden of making money, taking time that could be spent on your art. Worrying about getting behind on payments, having debt collectors begin to harass you, or losing your good credit rating can all increase your anxiety level, draining your creative energy in the process. Worries about debt can also cause you to feel guilty, and guilt is not conducive to creativity.

It's easy to see how people get into more debt than they can afford. We live in a culture that seems to accept being in debt as a normal part of life. The idea of saving up for a new (or used) car and paying cash rather than buying or leasing one on credit is out of date and almost unheard of. Despite recent years of unprecedented prosperity, low interest rates, high wages, and plentiful employment opportunities, studies show that individual consumers are more in debt today than ever before. The average wage earner is saving a smaller percentage of yearly income than in the history of this country. Adults are working longer hours for better wages, yet many have resigned themselves both to staying in the work force well beyond normal retirement age and to being in debt for the rest of their lives.

Nationally syndicated columnist Ellen Goodman writes about what is taken for granted as "normal life" here at the beginning of the twenty-first century. "Normal is getting dressed in clothes that you buy for work, driving through traffic in a car that you are still paying for, in order to get to the job that you need so you can pay for the clothes, car, and the house that you leave empty all day in order to afford to live in it."[4] What is going on here? Why do we so willingly shackle ourselves to a lifetime of debt just so we can possess more stuff we don't need—stuff that we have to store, maintain, eventually get rid of, and spend most of our lives trying to pay for? Is this any kind of life? Unfortunately, for many Americans, this is the only kind of life they've ever known.

C. S. Lewis had an interesting slant on how we get tangled in the consumerism trap. In *The Screwtape Letters,* the demon Screwtape has the job of mentoring his protégé Wormwood in ways of seducing humans to their eternal doom. Screwtape counsels Wormwood that by playing on their addiction to the pursuit of "prosperity," humans can be brought to their destruction. Screwtape tells Wormwood:

> Prosperity knits a man to the World. He feels that he is "finding his place in it," while really it is finding its place in him. His increasing reputation, his widening circle of acquaintances, his sense of importance, the growing pressure of absorbing and agreeable work, build up in him a sense of being really at home on earth, which is just what we want.

Lewis warns us that our concern with prosperity can cause us to become entangled with the world, and that entanglement blocks out the light of the Holy Spirit, the energy of creativity. Our time, money, and attention go outward toward making money rather than inward toward focusing on Christ. We tell ourselves, "As soon as I get the car paid off," "As soon as we retire the mortgage on the house," "As soon as we get the kids through college," "As soon as I get enough invested to see me safely through retirement," and on and on, but that day never comes because there is always another "as soon as." Although we may tell ourselves that money is only a tool to get us where we need to be to feel secure, in reality we become the tool of money. Francis Bacon wrote, "If money be not thy servant, it will be thy master. The covetous man cannot so properly be said to possess wealth, as that it may be said to possess him."

It is possible to provide well for yourself and your family without becoming enmeshed in the money chase. It is possible to buy only what you need, spend only what you have, and put aside a portion of what you earn for the things you will need in the future. It is possible, as Paul advises us in 1 Thessalonians 4:11-12 to "aspire to live quietly, to mind your own affairs, and to work with your hands...so that you may command the respect of outsiders, and be dependent on nobody" (RSV). Being debt-free means being dependent on God rather than the world. That kind of independence can give us the time and resources we need to really start practicing our art.

Debt-Buster Tips

Getting out of debt and changing your perspective toward money is not easy, but both can be done. It requires a strong commitment to paying off the debts you already have while resisting the temptation to get into new ones in the process. Here are some things you can do to achieve the security that only being debt-free can give you.

- Consolidate all consumer debt into one loan at the lowest interest available. That will mean only one payment per month rather than several.
- After you've consolidated, always pay more than the minimum required on you monthly bill. (Add on your interest and service charges to see exactly how much you are actually paying for what you purchased, and you will see the benefit of paying off debt as quickly as possible.) Until that debt is paid off, you are a slave to the credit card company, the modern day "company store."
- *Pay cash for everything* until you are running a zero balance on your *one* credit card. Then pay off the total balance every month. If you have a month when you can't pay off the entire balance, lock your credit card away until you are down to zero again. If you have trouble keeping your

monthly expenditures at a level you can pay off every month, cut up the credit card and use only cash.

- With the exception of your home mortgage, do not make any long-term credit purchases.

With prayer and commitment, you can get out and stay out of debt, whatever your income may be. Once you do, when things get tight financially, you will only have to cut back on your spending to keep your head above water rather than worrying about where the money for your payments will come from. Keep in mind, as always, that each time we free our minds from worry or anxiety, we give ourselves the gifts of time and concentration to apply to developing our art.

Spending Less

Samuel Johnson said, "Whatever you have, spend less." Another way to put it is, "Whatever you *make,* spend less." The idea sounds simple, but living that way is difficult. Americans spend more than they make in part because the media bombard us with a never-ending "want list." Couple the effectiveness of advertising with the easy availability of credit, and you have a recipe for financial slavery and a lifetime of pursuing the acquisition of "stuff." Elaine St. James writes that we could dramatically reduce our spending if we never buy something we can't pay for in full by the end of the month. She also advises us to never shop without a detailed list, never buy anything unless it's on the list, and never buy anything we didn't know existed until we saw it in a shop window.[5] I would also add that the less television you watch, the less likely you are to see advertisements that may tempt you to overspend.

Saving for What You Need

Once you get out of debt and start spending less than you make, you can start to save for the things that may require a significant outlay of cash. Here is one fairly painless way to do this: whenever a debt is paid off—an automobile loan, for example—take the monthly payment you had been making and deposit it into a savings account so that you will already have your next car paid for by the time you need it. Financial experts also advise "pay yourself first." Even a small automatic deduction from each paycheck into a savings account will grow into significant savings if you vow to leave it untouched and never use it for impulse buying. If you can discipline yourself to do this, not only will you have the money for those expenses for which you used to borrow money, but the money you are saving will also be earning interest as it sits in your account.

Once saving for what you need becomes a habit, even a compulsion, you will discover all kinds of ways to tuck away a little extra money here and there to build up a nice nest egg. I have found a way to save by using a credit card that gives a "cash back" dividend at the end of each year based on how much I've

EXERCISE 5: WHAT I WANT

We started this chapter by looking at what is important to us. We've discussed ways to declutter our lives by off-loading some of the less important things in our lives that take our time and attention. Finally, we have addressed the idea of simplifying by managing money more prudently. This final exercise can be ongoing, and it is a great topic for daybook entries whenever you find yourself tempted to spend money on things that you don't really need and that might just cause more complications in your life.

Think of something you have been just dying to buy. It might be anything from a new pair of athletic shoes to a new car or a remodeling job on your home. Do this exercise even if what you've been wanting is only a new outfit or a subscription to a magazine. In your daybook list all the reasons you should have this thing and all the charged on the card that year. I *always* pay off my card each month, no matter how high the balance is, so I never pay a penny of interest on what I charge. I get a nice itemized statement of my spending every month (quite helpful for budgeting, for seeing where I need to cut back, and for preparing my tax returns), and since the card carries no annual fee, I get all this convenience, plus a nice check at the end of the year, for free!

Keep your life free from love of money, and be content with what you have; for he has said, "I will never fail you nor forsake you."

—HEBREWS 13:5, RSV

Last year, however, when I received my check for almost one hundred dollars, I decided to take the company up on an option they offered for doubling

reasons you want it. Then list any reasons, especially those in the "I can't really afford it" category, why you shouldn't have it.

Now go to your calendar and find the date six weeks from the day you do this exercise. Write: "Buy car" or "Buy new pair of sandals" or whatever it is you want to purchase on that day six weeks away. If, by the time you get to that date, you still have the desire to buy the item and have figured out how to manage it financially, go ahead and buy it. Chances are you'll find that by delaying the purchase, you no longer feel the need to make it. If you still do feel compelled, the purchase is probably legitimate: You've given it a lot of thought, you will have had time to save for it, and you will be less likely to get into more debt in order to buy it. If you make this exercise a habit, your money worries will lessen. You'll experience a sense of control over your finances rather than feeling that they control you and how you have to spend your time.

my "cash back award" by applying it to coupons offered by various companies. The catch was that I had to spend those coupons within a certain period of time, and to do so meant paying for things I might not have bought had I not had the coupons. Having that deadline hanging over my head turned out to be another source of stress in my life. So this year when I received my check, I deposited it immediately into my savings account. The satisfaction of seeing my savings grow is worth much more to me than anything those coupons could buy.

By having some money set aside either for planned purchases or inevitable emergencies, you will know the freedom of a worry-free mind. You will eliminate financial anxiety from your life, and that priceless sense of tranquillity can translate into the confidence to practice your art. "'I know the plans I have for you,' declares the LORD, 'plans to prosper you and not to harm you, plans to give you hope and a future'" (Jeremiah 29:11). God wants to prosper us, to give us hope and a future. Learning to control our spending so we can build up our savings is an act of faith that God will meet our needs. We can certainly feel more hopeful about the future when we have some money put aside for emergencies or for the things we need to buy. Furthermore, learning to save is a giant step towards simplifying our lives as we discover the peace that comes from living with fewer things and putting off until we can afford them the things we do decide to buy.

"Simplifying is about letting go of status, material things, and excessive activity so you'll have more time and opportunity to engage in what's really important to you," writes Susan Pilgrim. "You can live a meaningful life—comfortably, peacefully, and simply."[6]

In *The Simple Living Guide,* author and publisher Janet Luhrs ties simplifying in with creativity by saying:

> Creativity means opening your box, tearing down the sides and
> stretching out to discover new ways of looking at and doing things
> that will improve your life. The less buried you are in debt, overcom-
> mitted time, and junk, the more freed up you are to think of innova-

tive solutions. What a delight to discover these new paths, and what a way to keep our energy renewed.[7]

This "opening your box, tearing down the sides and stretching out" means believing that God is calling you to a higher purpose, calling you to be a cocreator with him. Simplifying your life means taking a risk and trusting God to meet your needs as you answer his creative call.

And we know that in all things God works
for the good of those who love him, who
have been called according to his purpose.

—ROMANS 8:28

Think About
These Things

Show me your ways, O LORD, teach me your paths;
guide me in your truth and teach me, for you are God my Savior,
and my hope is in you all day long.

PSALM 25:4-5

You are coming to the end of this book, but not, I hope, to the end of your endeavors to make the life of an artist your own. The habits and practices you have been developing can become a part of you for the rest of your life.

The last exercise is an assignment that will bring to the conscious level the lessons and insights that have been most significant to you as you've read the book. By taking a look at what you considered important enough to write about in your daybook, you will see where the Holy Spirit has revealed important truths to you as you gave yourself over to breathing in his inspiration. (Note—You may opt to do this exercise as part of the suggested Artist's Retreat described in the appendix titled Commencement.)

As you work through the exercise, the most difficult part may be the narrowing of your choices down to three things only, but that is one of the themes of this book: narrowing down and making choices about what's important enough to focus on.

LOOKING BACK, MOVING ON

- Read through your entire daybook. Take your time and enjoy it. (Make this one of your breathing exercises by going off somewhere quiet and beautiful to do your reading.)
- Highlight whatever strikes you as particularly significant.
- Read back through what you have highlighted and choose the three things you want to take with you from this book. What is worth remembering? What would you like to go back and do again? Briefly describe your three "greatest hits." If you are doing this with a group, be ready to share your insights with your group at your final meeting or during your artists' retreat.

_____

_____

_____

_____

_____

_____

_____

_____

_____

_____

_____

When we come to the conclusion of any book or any course, we may find ourselves overflowing with resolution and inspiration. After a time, however, what struck us as so true and important when we were involved in the material is forgotten, and we return to our old familiar ways. But by choosing the three things you want to take with you from this book, you are practicing the art of simplifying your life. You are also improving the odds that what you've learned will stay with you. If these three ideals can alter your life so that the artist within you becomes more real, your life will be fuller than when you first opened this book.

Finally…whatever is true, whatever is honorable, whatever is just, whatever is pure, whatever is lovely, whatever is gracious, if there is any excellence, if there is anything worthy of praise, think about these things.
—PHILIPPIANS 4:8, RSV

We began *The Creative Call* with John's magnificent description of the beginning of time. I have chosen to end the book with these words written by Paul—words that comprise one of the most beautiful passages in all of literature. I've selected them because they epitomize for me what the simple life, the artistic life, means. It is as much a "mental set" as it is a set of choices about time, money, work, leisure, and possessions. Simplicity is purity; it connotes clarity, lucidity, the absence of complication or conflict. It connotes peace, serenity, and equanimity. Simplicity is the calm at the eye of the tempest, still water beside roaring rapids, a harbor amid stormy seas. It is the place artists go when they are so caught up in their art that the worries and cares of the day have ceased to exist for them.

The artist who is centered in the Holy Spirit will attend to "whatever is true…honorable…just…pure…lovely [and]…gracious." For "if there is any excellence, if there is anything worthy of praise," the artist, dying to self and opening up to the gentle leading of the Holy Spirit in order to serve the work, will "think about these things" and learn to live life playing by heart.

AN ARTIST'S RETREAT

*Our vocation is not simply to be, but to work together with God
in the creation of our own life, our own identity, our own destiny.*

—THOMAS MERTON, *New Seeds of Contemplation*

*E*ach time I work through this book alone or lead a group through a
Creative Call workshop, I find myself in a quandary. The experience is a
lot like reading a good novel: I can't wait to see how everything will turn out
at the end, yet I also hate for it to be over. At the end of any *Creative Call* study,
I feel committed to making changes in my life so that I'll continue paying
attention to the talents God has given me. If I do the book in the context of
a group, after spending eight weeks with other "creative callers," I've inevitably
become attached to the other group members, not only as my students, but as
my friends. The creative spirit has just begun to flow though many of them
after doing the chapters on making time and simplifying. Although I realize
that once the class ends, I'll have an extra evening to myself every week, thus
making more time and simplifying my life, I'm just not ready to "put down the
book" yet. That's why—alone, with a close friend or two, or with your *Creative
Call* group—one truly "inspired" way to end your study of this book is to make a
retreat.

WHY RETREAT WHEN WE'VE COME SO FAR?

Before you decide whether or not to plan or participate in a retreat as a finale to your *Creative Call* study, consider why individuals throughout time have seen retreats as an important tool for renewal. People make retreats for a number of reasons. Long before Christ spent his forty days in the wilderness, spiritual seekers would go on quarantine in order to remove themselves from the distractions of everyday life. (The word *quarantine* originally meant a period of forty days and only later came to mean "isolation.") This quarantine would be a time of prayer and fasting during which the retreatants hoped to hear the voice of God and achieve a clearer vision of how to live their lives. It was a time of doing penance for the sinful things they had done and for the good things they had left undone. These people hoped that they would return home after their forty days of solitude feeling renewed, resolving to do better, and committed to living the life God intended them to live. (They might also return several pounds lighter, although the popular belief that they took no food for forty days is probably true only in cases of extreme zealotry. Most people on quarantine ate every day after sundown, much as Moslems do today during Ramadan.)

There has recently been a renewed interest in personal retreats. Guesthouses at monasteries and facilities at retreat centers are often booked half a year in advance. People go on retreat for a day, a weekend, or even longer periods of time. For months at a time over the course of several years, writer Kathleen Norris lived in a Benedictine monastery as a layperson. She describes her experiences in her book *The Cloister Walk*. A friend of mine who is the pastor of a church in the town where I live goes to a Trappist monastery each year for a week of silent retreat in order to renew his spirit and listen to God without the demands and distractions of running a church. I know people who plan yearly retreats just as they do their annual vacations. However long you choose to go on retreat, the purpose of your going is to hear from and to speak to God without the interruptions of daily life. It will also be a time to formalize your commitment to practicing the artistic talents God has given you.

THE PURPOSEFUL RETREAT

A *retreat* is "a period of seclusion, retirement or solitude" or "a period of withdrawal for prayer, meditation, and study." To go on retreat is to sculpt out the time to experience "a place affording peace, quiet, privacy or security." A retreat can provide closure on the good work the Lord has begun in you as you read and worked through *The Creative Call.* This special time of solitude, silence, and/or fellowship can give you a vision about where to go from here. That's why I called this chapter Commencement rather than Appendix or Epilogue. *Commencement* means "beginning." The marvelous thing about deciding to end the course with a retreat is that you will actually be finishing the study with a ceremony of commencement: a sacred time to mark the commencement of your life as a more creative individual.

The purpose of your artist's retreat will be twofold. First, the retreat will culminate your study of *The Creative Call* with some quiet, quality time so that you can read back through your daybook and process what you have learned. You will seek to hear what God wants to reveal to you about the way in which you should go forward in your life as an artist. Second, the retreat will help you create and experience your own ritual, like a graduation ceremony, which we will call our Ceremony of Appointment, described in detail later in this chapter.

If you have put time and energy into reading and working through this book, you deserve to give yourself the gift of going on a retreat. Some readers may be thinking, "I just can't make the time to do this. I'm a single mom working full time, and I just can't get away for a weekend retreat." If you go back to chapters 7 and 8, I think you'll see what my response is to that kind of thinking. Even if you make only four hours on a day when the kids are in school, you can still retreat from the world for a period of time. If you are not in a group, you might go alone or with a close friend to a nearby park or wilderness area. Getting away from your house and place of employment and spending some quality time thinking about what you've learned throughout the course of this book can do much toward solidifying your resolve to become the artist God designed you to be. In order for me to take time from my too-busy life to make a retreat, I have to know the experience will include three main elements: seclusion, solitude, and significance.

Seclusion. I have to go far enough away from home that I can only be called back to my normal life for a real emergency. The setting has to be pleasant and inviting, and, if possible, a place that has been designed for retreats. This kind of setting means that food and housing issues will be provided, and it usually means there will be great places to walk, sit, write, meditate, and pray. Although the location doesn't have to be away from the city, I personally have a better retreat experience when I go to a retreat center in the woods, at the beach, in the mountains, by a lake, or at a monastery. A dramatic change from my everyday scenery seems to enhance the retreat experience for me.

Solitude. I have to have lots of alone time at a retreat, even if I go with a group. Many retreats I've attended have been so overbooked with activities, speakers, workshops, and worship services that I return home more exhausted than when I left. A good group retreat will allow each participant to spend a great deal of time alone—in his or her room if it is an overnight event or wandering about the grounds of the facility undisturbed.

Each person should respect the others' need for solitude and silence. A retreat should not end up being a therapy session for one person at the expense of others. Activities should encourage personal growth, but for our purposes, the retreat will *not* be a time to listen to and process each other's personal problems. This should be a time of intimacy between each person and God. That kind of intimacy requires periods of solitude. If you are going on retreat by yourself, getting the solitude you need will not be an issue. However, if you worked through this book with a group and are going on retreat together, make sure everyone is clear about how you will each respect one another's right to solitude.

Significance. If you decide to make a retreat by yourself after doing *The Creative Call,* you will have a marvelous opportunity to experience a significant time alone with God. You can take time to read through your eight weeks of day-book entries, write about all the things you didn't have time to write about before, pray, talk to God, and listen to what God has to say to you about doing your art. Few of us ever take a weekend or more to be alone, so being bold enough to make a solitary retreat will be significant in and of itself. If you decide to go with a group, the group activities you choose will have to be meaningful, purposeful, and not just "fillers." I like being offered structured activities, but I prefer a certain amount of personal choice as to whether or not to participate in them. A person on retreat should never feel pressured to perform or to participate if what that person needs is just to be alone with God.

If you are planning to go as a group, share your ideas ahead of time about what is important to you. This openness in advance will help make the experience one that you will look forward to and enjoy. If you are going by yourself, you might still want to make the list below to avoid the pitfalls of overbooking your retreat time with things you really don't want or need to do. You may want to use the spaces below to make a list of the positives you would like to experience and the negatives you hope to avoid.

Positives I Would Like to Experience   **Negatives I Hope to Avoid**

_____   _____

_____   _____

_____   _____

_____   _____

_____   _____

_____   _____

_____   _____

_____   _____

Use this list to plan the kind of retreat experiences that will be the most valuable for you and/or your group.

PUTTING IT ALL TOGETHER

This section covers key considerations in planning for a successful Creative Call Retreat. Those of you who have read *The Creative Call* on your own rather than studied it as a group may find that some of the suggestions in the rest of this chapter do not apply to you. But if you like the idea of having a ritual or ceremony in which you make a commitment to spending time practicing your art from now on, you may consider inviting a friend or two to go on your retreat with you. They don't necessarily have to read the book beforehand, but it will help if they do. Anyone whom you feel comfortable with and who also has a desire to get away and spend some time alone with God can go along with you.

A Sacred Space

Try to choose a place for your retreat that is easily accessible and that can accommodate the various schedules of the retreatants. Several good retreat centers are within an hour's drive from where I live. These centers are close enough to allow the option of having the retreat for one day only, but they are far enough away to make it worth one's while to spend the night. If you or people in your group want to discourage calls from home because someone can't find the mayonnaise, then I suggest choosing a spot that is at least an hour away. It's also a good idea to leave the cell phones behind or in the car, turned off. Remember the days before cell phones? It's still possible to live with a check-in call when you arrive and an emergency number at home just for that: emergencies. Otherwise, you'll be getting calls about such earth-shattering matters as, "Dad, Bobby's making fun of my braces!"

(Again) the Question of Time

Decide how much time you want to allow for this retreat. If you are going as a group, you may wish to base your decision on a consensus about what the people in your group want to have happen during this special time together. I suggest four activities for your group to consider:

- time alone with your daybook
- a couple of artist workshop activities if that is how your group is geared
- the Ceremonies of Appointment (described below) as part of a closing time of worship
- if you spend the night and are with a group, you can also have some fun socializing

Think about the two questions below and write down your response on the lines provided.

How much time do I want to spend alone with my journal, with my own private thoughts, in prayer, or relaxing and napping?

_____

_____

_____

As part of your retreat experience, I suggest you allow yourself two or three hours to read through and highlight your entire artist daybook. Then write about what you learned from your study of *The Creative Call.* You may want to use the exercise (Looking Back, Moving On) in chapter 8 as a guideline. If you are on a group retreat, allow adequate time for talking about what each person learned from doing this exercise.

Do we want to include any creative hands-on activities during the retreat?

_____

_____

Several people in your group might be willing to conduct one- or two-hour workshops using their talent to teach others a form of art that might not be the other people's usual focus. I have been to several writing retreats with Jan A. Richardson, a visual artist, author, and friend, and she always includes writing about specific topics and then illustrating our writing through collage, drawing, or painting. It's not exactly an art class any more than the retreat is a writing class. But it does provide writers an opportunity to express themselves through a different medium than the written word, and, likewise, visual artists are given a chance to explore the written word as a medium of expression.

During your retreat, visual artists might want to attend a small-group session on the specifics of writing autobiography or on creative journaling or poetry writing. Writers, excited to be getting their hands into something more solid than words for a change, might enjoy a session where they hand-make a piece of pottery. A computer expert might take a couple of people at a time and show them how to use PhotoShop or Paint. Or, participants could bring all kinds of "found objects" with them to create a mixed media piece, an activity that several artists in your group can help coach. Poll the people in your group and see if even one or two people would be willing to lead a session. Base at least part of your decision about how long your retreat will be on how many activities you can actually expect to have and how much interest there is in those activities. I suggest you allow at least three hours for this component of the retreat, more or less depending on how many workshops you intend to do.

If you are going on your retreat alone, you might want to pick up some art supplies to take with you. Use part of your time to experiment with a medium you are not used to working with but have always wanted to investigate. This could start you down a new avenue of creative expression. *Drawing on the Right Side of the Brain* is a great book to use for getting your feet wet as a neophyte visual artist. (See Suggested Reading at the back of this book.)

Another way to bring closure to your *Creative Call* study and to your retreat is the Ceremony of Appointment. We'll turn to this idea now.

THE CEREMONY OF APPOINTMENT

It was near the end of my twenty-third year of teaching. My fifth graders were reading *The Giver,* by Lois Lowry, as a culminating activity for their semester-long "future studies" unit in their gifted class. In this futuristic novel about a "kinder, gentler" but totalitarian society, the main character, Jonas, goes through a rite of passage called the Ceremony of the Twelves. During this ritual the elders of the community, whose job it is to pay attention to each child's aptitudes, talents, and abilities from infancy on, give every twelve-year-old his or her assignment for life. Once this assignment is made, all future education and life experiences are directed toward preparing the child for his or her vocation. Of course, as in most science-fiction novels, the price for this kind of job security and "correct" career placement is giving up the right to choose your vocation for yourself. This was a major theme of the book: What price are you willing to pay for an "ideal" society?

What interested me most that particular year was my students' responses to the idea of society's choosing the career paths for its young people. Despite the oppressive nature of the system portrayed in this book, my students didn't respond to it as negatively as I'd expected. In fact, one girl even asked if we could create our own Ceremony of the Twelves after we finished the book. The class agreed that they would really like to have a ceremony in their own lives where they could receive some guidance about their future. So, as a concluding project to mark the end of our future studies unit and the end of my students' elementary-school years, each student devised his or her own Ceremony of the Twelves.

They planned ceremonies that would reflect their own personalities, what was important to them, and what they saw as their emerging talents and aptitudes. "What would a ceremony marking the end of childhood and the advent of adulthood be like?" I asked them to consider. They all brought various elements for their ceremonies to class on Ceremony of the Twelves day—some combination of candles, food, incense, photographs, flowers, books, music, awards, favorite toys, and trophies. Each one decided what should be on his or her table or "altar." They selected music, readings, and food; they organized the order of events in their ceremonies and wrote out a script for the people they drafted to participate in the ritual with them. One part of their rite had to include symbolically putting away several items that symbolized the childhood they were leaving behind and then unpacking some objects that stood for what they intended to take with them into their "new life." They placed all of these items on their altar, explaining as they went what each article symbolized for them.

The students designated someone to be the "elder," the one who would give them a symbol of their appointment for the rest of their life and a commission to go out and pursue that vocation or calling. (We chose to call this person the "elder" because that was what the people who gave out the assignments in *The Giver* were called.) For example, a person who had musical talent might be given a musical instrument or some sheet music along with the admonition to go into the world and become a great musician. Someone who hoped to become a professional athlete might be given a basketball or a baseball bat and instructed to practice hard in order to become a great ball player. A computer whiz had his friend hand him a mouse and keyboard as symbols of his appointment to become a successful computer engineer.

At the end of each person's ceremony, the rest of us surrounded him or her, raised our hands, and, despite this being a public school classroom, I led them in a short prayer for that person's hopes, dreams, and future. The activity was very powerful for them and for me. It confirmed what I was becoming convinced of as I was writing this book: that we are all hungry for a sense of direction, a clear calling, a perfect fit that will give meaning and purpose to our lives.

APPOINTMENT WITH GOD

I believe God calls each of us to intimacy with him. He knows who we are, he gives us the talents and abilities we were born with, and he knows what we need to do with those talents in order to live a life that is pleasing to him and fulfilling for us. We read in Psalm 139:13-14: "For you created my inmost being; you knit me together in my mother's womb. I praise you because I am fearfully and wonderfully made; your works are wonderful, I know that full well." It is wonderful to me that the Lord of creation is so intimately interested in my personal growth that he has laid out a plan for my life for me to follow. Our talents, as I have suggested throughout this book, are road signs God gives each of us, pointing us toward fulfillment and intimacy with him.

I took you from the ends of the earth, from its farthest corners I called you. I said, "You are my servant"; I have chosen you and have not rejected you.

—ISAIAH 41:9

Some people object to the idea that God might have a plan for our lives. The implication is that there is only one way we can go in life that is pleasing to God, and if we deviate from that straight and narrow path, we will irreversibly mess up our lives. They see the concept of "God's plan" as being akin to having their free will taken from them. That's not how I see it. The fact that we have been given free will is proof that God wants us to choose him, rather than just blindly do as we're told. We choose our own paths throughout our lives, and God provides many forms of guidance along the way so that we can make the best choices. I believe that the purpose of our struggling to improve ourselves is to become more Christlike, and one key to spiritual maturity lies in recognizing our gifts and talents, using them to glorify God, and developing rather than burying them. God planned for us to have these talents, and he offers us the chance to use them in order to know him better and to glorify him through the works of our hands.

Some of us are especially fortunate. With encouragement and direction from those who know and love us best and with a clear understanding about what

having a personal relationship with God means, we learn at an early age to culti-
vate and nourish our artistic abilities. We can accept, perhaps only at the unconscious level, that these talents are a part of God's efforts to give good gifts to us so
that, in turn, we can give them back to the world. But most of us have to get
some experience behind us before we see that our gifts are not merely a distraction, but are instead a direction marker, pointing us—and those we come in con-
tact with—to God. This is what I mean by God having a plan for our lives.

In 1 Timothy 4:14-16 we are admonished, "Do not neglect your gift, which
was given you through a prophetic message when the body of elders laid their
hands on you. Be diligent in these matters; give yourself wholly to them, so that
everyone may see your progress. Watch your life and doctrine closely. Persevere in
them, because if you do, you will save both yourself and your hearers." This passage gained a new and more pertinent meaning for me after my fifth-graders'
Ceremony of the Twelves. When I heard those words, I wondered if many of us
aren't still waiting for "the body of elders [to lay] their hands" on us, still waiting
for our gifts to be acknowledged and encouraged. Is one reason there are so many
"dis-appointed" middle-aged adults because somewhere along the road of life,
many of us missed receiving that appointment, or anointing, from God? Do we,
like my young students, crave some ritual or ceremony that might indicate in a
public way what we already know in our hearts, that we are God's artists and
should live our lives as though we are?

Confirmation, Bar Mitzvah, and Bat Mitzvah are ceremonies that Christian
and Jewish communities have used throughout the ages to mark the advent of
adulthood. These celebrations allow young people to publicly proclaim their reli-
gious convictions, but they now have little to do with helping children recognize
their calling or vocation. In the past, not only the extended family, but the entire
community would watch, encourage, and nurture a child as he or she grew up.
By the time he or she reached twelve or thirteen years of age, the village that it
takes to raise a child had a pretty good idea of what that child's vocation or calling would be. The child's caregivers would guide the child into the vocation for

which he or she seemed best suited. This decision would determine what course the child's life would take from that point: further education, an apprenticeship, job placement, or maybe even a betrothal. Although most of us are repelled by the absence of personal choice that is inherent in a system like this, we might do well to ask ourselves how well we've done making these choices on our own.

We can't go back to adolescence to keep that appointment with God, to have that ceremony where we are given permission and encouragement to use our art and develop our talents, but I believe it is not only therapeutic, but spiritually powerful for us as adults to seek out that appointment now. It isn't too late to come together with other artists, to make the commitment to respond to our creative call, and to ask God first to speak to us through our group and then to give us the anointing we wish we'd received when we were younger. I propose that either on your own, with a trusted friend, or with your *Creative Call* small group, you create your Ceremony of Appointment as a way of reaching closure in your study of *The Creative Call.*

Your Ceremony of Appointment can take many forms. Like my students, you may want to begin with a reading by someone in your group, or by the friend you've brought on your individual retreat, stating the purpose of the ceremony: to give you your appointment or assignment as an artist for the rest of your life. Once you give this concept some thought, you will undoubtedly come up with favorite bits of poetry, songs, scripture, and writing of your own to flesh out and personalize your ceremony. Think about other meaningful ceremonies you've attended (baptisms, confirmations, weddings, ordinations, induction ceremonies for honorary societies, graduations, and so on) and see if you can't incorporate some of the elements of these into your Ceremony of Appointment. Remember that this ceremony is about formalizing your commitment to begin answering the creative call and practicing your art. Keep in mind that your ceremony will look different from anyone else's.

In the first ceremony like this that I participated in, I asked my friend Louise to act as leader so I could be given the appointment. The ceremony included poetry, prayers, Scripture reading, and the lighting of candles to symbolize God's lighting the path of my awakening as an artist. Towards that end, Louise said to me: "Be an artist, Janice. Follow your dreams; use your gifts. Let the meditations of your heart and the words of your pen be pleasing to God, your Rock and your Redeemer. This is what you were created to do. Do it in hope, and joy, and humility." We then read a poem by Clair of Assisi and closed with the giving of gifts. My gifts included a blank book, a fountain pen, and a new book of sheet music for the piano.

You may want to use some of these ideas in your own ceremony, or you may want to make up a ceremony that is entirely your own. You might want to include some of the prayers and poems found in the appendix. If you are comfortable doing so, taking Communion together is a lovely way to wrap up the retreat.

Use your imagination, your gifts, your talents, and the guidance of the Holy Spirit to create the kind of retreat that is just what you, as an individual or group, want and need. Call down the Holy Spirit of God in both the planning and the making of the retreat. End with a time of prayer that unites everyone in the commitment to begin living a more artistic life—not to glorify yourselves, but to glorify the One who dwells within us and calls us his own.

May I be worthy to do it! Lord, make me
crystal clear for thy light to shine through.
—KATHERINE MANSFIELD

PRAYERS

*L*ike poems, prayers can convey in a few well-chosen words thoughts and feelings with which others can identify. When we read the prayers of others, we can be drawn closer to God. Whether you are comfortable with spontaneous prayer or with written prayers, you may find the words of some of the following great "pray-ers" meaningful to you. May the following collection enrich your prayer life as you seek to follow your creative call.

PRAYER OF PETITION

Almighty and everlasting God, you are always more ready
    to hear than we to pray, and to give more than we either desire
    or deserve;
Pour upon us the abundance of your mercy, forgiving us those things
    of which our conscience is afraid, and giving us those good
    things for which we are not worthy to ask, except through the merits
    and mediation of
Jesus Christ our Savior, who lives and reigns with you and the
    Holy Spirit,
one God, forever and ever.
    —*The Book of Common Prayer*

ACT OF CONTRITION

O my God, I am heartily sorry for having offended Thee,
and I detest all my sins because of Thy just punishments,
but most of all because they offend Thee, my God,
Who art all-good and deserving of all my love.
I firmly resolve, with the help of Thy grace, to sin no more
and to avoid the near occasions of sin.

    —Roman Catholic

VENI, SANCTE SPIRITUS

Come, Holy Spirit, and send out a ray of your heavenly light.
Come, father of the poor, come, giver of gifts, come, light of our hearts.
Come, kindly comforter, sweet guest of our soul and sweet freshness.
Rest in hardship, moderation in the heat, relief in pain!
O most blessed light, fill the innermost hearts of those who
    believe in you.
Without your divine power there is nothing in man,
nothing that is harmless.
Wash what is unclean, water what is arid, heal what is wounded.
Bend what is stiff, warm what is cold, guide what has gone astray.
Give to those who believe in you and trust in you your seven sacred gifts.
Give the reward of virtue, give the end of salvation, give
    lasting happiness!

    —The author of this sequence, which dates to the beginning of the
      thirteenth century, is probably Stephen Langton, c. 1155-1228,
      Archbishop of Canterbury during the reign of King John.

CONFORM MY WILL TO YOURS

Lord, let me not henceforth desire health or life except to spend
them for you, with you, and in you. You alone know what is good
for me; do therefore what seems best to you. Give to me or take
from me; conform my will to yours; and grant that with humble and
perfect submission and in holy confidence I may receive the orders
of your eternal providence, and may equally adore all that comes
to me from you.

—Blaise Pascal, 1623-1662

LET NOTHING DISTURB THEE

Let nothing disturb thee,   Nada te turbe,

Nothing affright thee;   Nada te espante;

All things are passing,   Todo se pasa,

God never changeth!   Dios no se muda.

Patient endurance   La paciencia todo

Attaineth to all things;   lo alcanza.

Who God possesseth   Quien a Dios tiene

In nothing is wanting;   Nada le falta.

Alone God sufficeth.   Solo Dios basta.

— These lines were found in the breviary of Saint Teresa of Avila
  after her death in 1582. Friar Gracián wrote, "This breviary
  belonged to Mother Teresa of Jesus, and she was using it for her
  prayers when God called her to heaven from Alba. And because
  this is true, I have signed it with my name: Fray Gerónimo
  Gracián de la Madre de Dios."

THE HOLY BREATH

Holy Spirit, which with thy holy breath cleans men's minds,

comforting them when they be in sorrow,

cheering them up with pure gladness when they be in heaviness,

leading them into all truth when they be out of the way,

kindling in them the fire of charity when they be cold,

knitting them together with the glue of peace when

    they be at variance,

and garnishing and enriching them with sundry gifts…

I beseech thee, maintain thy gifts in me,

and increase the things daily,

which thou hast vouchsafed to bestow upon me,

that by thy governance the lusts of the flesh may die

    more and more in me

and the desire of heavenly life more quicken and increase.

Let me so pass through the misty desert of this world

by thy light going before me

as I may neither be defiled with Satan's wiles,

nor be entangled with any errors disagreeing from thy truth.

    —Desiderius Erasmus, 1466-1536

DIRECT AND RULE OUR HEARTS

God, forasmuch as without thee we are not able to please thee,
mercifully grant that thy Holy Spirit may in all things direct and
rule our hearts.

    —*The Book of Common Prayer*

CELTIC BLESSING I

May the God of gentleness be with you,

caressing you with sunlight and rain,

caressing you with rain and wind.

May His tenderness shine through you,

to warm all those who are hurt and alone.

May the God of strength be with you,

holding you in strong-fingered hands.

May you be a sacrament of His strength

to those whose hands you hold.

May the God of gentleness be with you,

caressing you with sunlight and rain,

caressing you with rain and wind. Amen.

AN OFFERING OF ONESELF

Lord Jesus, I give you my hands to do your work.

I give you my feet to go your way.

I give you my eyes to see as you see.

I give you my tongue to speak your words.

I give you my mind that you may think in me.

I give you my spirit that you may pray in me.

Above all, I give you my heart that I may love the

    Father and all humankind.

I give you my whole self that you may grow in me, so that you, Lord,

May be the one who lives and works and prays in me. Amen.

    —Author unknown

THEREFORE, LET US WORK

Therefore, let us work, let us develop all our possibilities;

not for ourselves, but for our fellow-creatures.

Let us be enlightened in our efforts,

Let us strive after the general welfare of humanity and
    indeed of all creation.

We are born here to do certain things.

Life may be misery or not;

it concerns us not; let us do what we have to do.

    —Soyen Shaku, Japan, 1859-1919

PRAYER TO THE HOLY SPIRIT

Spirit of wisdom and understanding,

enlighten our minds to perceive

the mysteries of the universe in relation to eternity.

Spirit of right judgment and courage, guide us and make us firm

in our baptismal decision to follow Jesus' way of love.

Spirit of knowledge and reverence,

help us to see the lasting value of justice and mercy

in our everyday dealings with one another.

May we respect life as we work to solve problems

of family and nation, economy and ecology.

Spirit of God, spark our faith, hope and love into new action each day.

Fill our lives with wonder and awe

in your presence which penetrates all creation.

Amen.

    —Roman Catholic

CELTIC BLESSING II

The grace of God be yours.

The grace of love be with yours.

The grace of home be yours.

The grace of hearth be yours.

The grace and pride of faith be yours.

The grace of the God of life be yours.

The grace of the loving Christ be yours.

The grace of the Holy Spirit be yours.

God to cherish you.

God to hold you.

God to enfold you.

The Three be about your head.

The Three be about your breast.

The Three be about your body.

Each night and each day, in the enfolding of the Three,

throughout thy life long, forever and ever.

Amen.

GIVE US GRACE

O Lord, give us grace we beseech Thee, to hear and obey thy
voice which saith to every one of us, "This is the way. Walk ye in
it." Nevertheless, let us not hear it behind us saying, "This is the
way;" but rather before us saying, "follow me." When Thou puttest
us forth, go before us; when the way is too great for us, carry us; in the
darkness of death, comfort us; in the day of resurrection, satisfy us.

—Christina Georgina Rossetti, 1828-1882

NINA'S PRAYER

Dear Holy Spirit, thank you for the many blessings and creative gifts you have already bestowed upon me. I yield myself to you that you would anoint me, according to your divine intentions and for your glory, with your empowering presence—that I would be all you have created me to be, and that I would do all you have created me to do. Even as I am yielding to your guidance and inspiration, I ask you to purify my motives, thoughts, emotions and intentions. Amen.

—Nina Snyder, American artist and writer, 2000

PRAYER FOR ONE'S CALLING

Almighty God, our heavenly Father,
Who declares Your glory and shows forth Your handiwork
in the heavens and in the earth;
Deliver us, we beseech You, in our several callings,
from the service of mammon,
That we may do the work which You give us to do,
in truth, in beauty, and in righteousness,
with singleness of heart as thy servants,
and to the benefit of our fellow men;
For the sake of Him who came among us as One that serves,
Your Son Jesus Christ our Lord.

—*The Book of Common Prayer*

ABOUND IN YOU

Sever me from myself that I may be grateful to you;

may I perish to myself that I may be safe in you;

may I die to myself that I may live in you;

may I wither to myself that I may blossom in you;

may I be emptied of myself that I may abound in you;

may I be nothing to myself that I may be all to you.

—Desiderius Erasmus, 1466-1536

FIRE OF THE SPIRIT

Fire of the Spirit, life of the lives of creatures,

spiral of sanctity, bond of all natures,

glow of charity, light of clarity,

taste of sweetness to sinners—

be with us and hear us.

Composer of all things,

light of all the risen,

key of salvation,

release from the dark prison,

hope of all unions, scope of chastities,

joy in the glory, strong honor—

be with us and hear us.

—Hildegard of Bingen, 1098-1179

TAKE MY LIFE

Take my life and let it be consecrated, Lord, to thee;
Take my moments and my days, let them flow in ceaseless praise;
Let them flow in ceaseless praise.

Take myself and I will be ever, only, all for thee.
Take my hands and let them move at the impulse of thy love;
At the impulse of thy love.

Take my feet and let them be swift and beautiful for thee.
Take myself and I will be ever, only, all for thee;
Ever, only, all for thee.

Take my voice and let me sing ever, only, for my King.
Take my lips and let them be filled with messages from thee;
Filled with messages from thee.

Take myself and I will be ever, only, all for thee.
Take my silver and my gold, not a mite would I withhold;
Not a mite would I withhold.

Take my intellect and use ev'ry pow'r as thou shalt choose.
Take myself and I will be ever, only, all for thee;
Ever, only, all for thee.

Take my will and make it thine, it shall be no longer mine.
Take my heart it is thine own, it shall be thy royal throne;
It shall be thy royal throne.

Take my love, my Lord, I pour at thy feet my treasure store;
Take myself and I will be ever, only, all for thee.
Ever, only, all for thee.
                —Frances Ridley Havergal, 1836-1879

PRAYER TO THE HOLY SPIRIT

I am going to reveal to you the secret of sanctity
    and happiness.
Every day for five minutes control your imagination
and close your eyes to the things of sense
and your ears to all the noises of the world,
in order to enter into yourself.
Then, in the sanctity of your baptized soul
(which is the temple of the Holy Spirit)
speak to that Divine Spirit, saying to Him:
"Oh, Holy Spirit, beloved of my soul…
    I adore you.
Enlighten me, guide me, strengthen me,
    console me.
Tell me what I should do; give me Your orders.
I promise to submit myself to all that You
    desire of me
and to accept all that You permit to happen to me.
Let me only know Your will."
If you do this, your life will flow along happily,
    serenely,
and full of consolation, even in the midst of trials.
Grace will be proportioned to the trial, giving
    you the strength to carry it
and you will arrive at the gate of Paradise,
laden with merit.
This submission to the Holy Spirit is the secret
    of sanctity.
    —Cardinal Mercier, 1851-1926

GO FORWARD SECURELY

What you hold, may you always hold.

What you do, may you always do and never abandon.

But with swift pace, light step, and unswerving feet,

so that even your steps stir up no dust,

Go forward securely, joyfully and swiftly, on the path

    of prudent happiness,

believing nothing, agreeing with nothing

which would dissuade you from this resolution

or which would place a stumbling block for you on the way,

so that you may offer your vow to the Most High

in the pursuit of that perfection to which the Spirit of the

    Lord has called you.

    —Clair of Assisi, 1194-1253

NOTES

Chapter Two: Listening

1. Madeleine L'Engle, *Walking on Water: Reflections on Faith and Art* (Wheaton, Ill.: Harold Shaw, 1980), 12.

2. L'Engle, *Walking on Water*, 16.

3. Dorothea Brande, *Becoming a Writer* (London: Macmillan, 1996), 65-6.

4. Mihaly Csikszentmihalyi, *Creativity: Flow and the Psychology of Discovery and Invention* (New York: HarperCollins, 1997), 347.

5. Deena Metzger, *Writing for Your Life: A Guide and Companion to the Inner Worlds* (London: HarperCollins, 1992), 23.

Chapter Three: Awakening

1. Joanna Laufer and Kenneth S. Lewis, *Inspired: the Breath of God* (New York: Doubleday, 1998), 84-8.

2. L'Engle, *Walking on Water*, 76-7.

3. L'Engle, *Walking on Water*, 149.

Chapter Four: Forgiving

1. "If You Can Dream It," *Guideposts*, October 1998, 6.

2. See 2 Samuel 11. See also Psalms 51 and 32. *The NIV Life Application Bible* (Grand Rapids, Mich.: Zondervan, 1991), 935, 959, gives helpful footnotes for David's prayer of confession and his praise song of forgiveness.

3. See Matthew 6:12.

4. Laufer and Lewis, *Inspired*, 166-7.

5. Laufer and Lewis, *Inspired*, 167.

Chapter Five: Breathing In

1. Madeleine L'Engle, *And It Was Good: Reflections on Beginnings* (Wheaton, Ill.: Harold Shaw, 1983), 80.

2. Laufer and Lewis, *Inspired*, 82.

3. Laufer and Lewis, *Inspired*, 88.

4. Anne Lamott, *Bird by Bird: Some Instructions on Writing and Life* (New York: Anchor, 1994) 100-1.

5. Marshall Cook, *Freeing Your Creativity: A Writer's Guide* (Cincinnati: Writer's Digest, 1992), 56.

6. Julia Cameron, *The Artist's Way* (New York: Putnam, 1992), 18.

7. Cook, *Freeing Your Creativity*, 65.

Chapter Six: Breathing Out

1. L'Engle, *Walking on Water*, 18.

2. Natalie Goldberg, *Wild Mind: Living the Writer's Life* (New York: Bantam, 1986), 45.

3. Franky Schaeffer, *Addicted to Mediocrity: 20th Century Christians and the Arts* (Wheaton, Ill.: Crossway, 1981), 60.

4. Schaeffer, *Mediocrity*, 60

Chapter 7: Making Time

1. Ann McGee-Cooper, *Time Management for Unmanageable People* (New York: Bantam, 1994), 67.

2. Cook, *Freeing Your Creativity*, 51.

3. Anne Morrow Lindbergh, *Gift from the Sea* (New York: Pantheon, 1977), 115.

4. See Charles Hummel at http://www.cyber-nation.com.

5. L'Engle, *Walking on Water*, 122.

Chapter 8: Simplifying

1. See Susan Pilgrim, *InSync® Resources for Changing Your Life*, http://www.livinginsync.com/page6.htm.

2. Elaine St. James, *Living the Simple Life* (New York: Hyperion, 1996).

3. Steven Catlin, *Work Less and Play More* (Ventura, Calif.: Kimberlite, 1997), 112-3.

4. Ellen Goodman, "The Cloud on Your Vacation That Gets Darker and Darker," *Boston Globe,* 22 August 1993, Op-Ed section, 73.

5. For more money-saving tips, see Elaine St. James, *Simplify Your Work Life* (New York: Hyperion, 2001).

6. Susan Pilgrim, *InSync® Resources,* 6.

7. Janet Luhrs, *The Simple Living Guide* (New York: Broadway, 1997), 164.

SUGGESTED READING

Aldrich, Anne Hazard. *Notes from Myself: A Guide to Creative Journal Writing.* New York: Carroll & Graf, 1998.

Babb, Fred. *Go to Your Studio and Make Stuff: The Fred Babb Poster Book.* New York: Workman, 1998.

Brande, Dorothea. *Becoming a Writer.* London: Macmillan, 1996.

Brehony, Kathleen A. *Awakening at Midlife.* New York: Riverhead, 1996.

Briner, Bob. *Roaring Lambs: A Gentle Plan to Radically Change Your World.* Grand Rapids: Zondervan, 1993.

Cameron, Julia. *The Artist's Way: A Spiritual Path to Higher Creativity.* New York: Jeremy P. Tarcher/Putnam, 1992.

Catlin, Steven. *Work Less and Play More.* Ventura, Calif.: Kimberlite, 1997.

Common Service Book of the Lutheran Church. The United Lutheran Church in America, 1918.

Cook, Marshall. *Freeing Your Creativity: A Writer's Guide.* Cincinnati: Writer's Digest, 1992.

Csikszentmihalyi, Mihaly. *Creativity: Flow and the Psychology of Discovery and Invention.* New York: HarperCollins, 1997.

Edwards, Betty. *Drawing on the Right Side of the Brain: A Course in Enhancing Creativity and Artistic Confidence,* Revised Edition. New York: Jeremy P. Tarcher/Putnam, 1989.

Ford-Grabowsky, Mary. *Prayers for All People.* New York: Doubleday, 1995.

Goldberg, Natalie. *Writing Down the Bones.* Boston: Shambhala, 1986.

———. *Wild Mind: Living the Writer's Life.* New York: Bantam, 1986.

Hoover, Rev. Hugo H. *Saint Joseph Daily Missal.* New York: Catholic Book Publishing, 1956.

"If You Can Dream It." *Guideposts,* October 1998.

Lamott, Anne. *Bird by Bird: Some Instructions of Writing and Life.* New York: Anchor, 1994.

———. *Travelling Mercies: Some Thoughts on Faith.* New York: Pantheon, 1999.

Laufer, Joanna and Kenneth S. Lewis. *Inspired: The Breath of God.* New York: Doubleday, 1998.

L'Engle, Madeleine. *And It Was Good: Reflections on Beginnings.* Wheaton, Ill.: Harold Shaw, 1983.

———. *Walking on Water: Reflections of Faith and Art.* Wheaton, Ill.: Harold Shaw, 1980, 1998, 2001.

Lindbergh, Anne Morrow. *Gifts from the Sea.* New York: Pantheon, 1977.

Luhrs, Janet. *The Simple Living Guide.* New York: Broadway, 1997.

Madden, Chris Casson. *A Room of Her Own: Women's Personal Spaces.* New York: Random House, 1997.

McGee-Cooper, Ann. *Time Management for Unmanageable People.* New York: Bantam, 1994.

Merton, Thomas. *New Seeds of Contemplation.* New York: New Directions, 1961.

Milton, John. *Complete Poems and Major Prose,* ed. Merritt Y. Hughes. New York: Odyssey, 1957.

Moran, Victoria. *Shelter for the Spirit.* New York: HarperCollins, 1997.

Pilgrim, Susan. *InSync® Resources For Changing Your Life.* http://www.livingin-sync.com/page6.htm#Simplifying

Pollack, Constance and Daniel Pollack, ed. *The Book of Uncommon Prayer.* Dallas: Word, 1996.

Richardson, Jan L. *In Wisdom's Path.* Cleveland: The Pilgrim Press, 2000.

Ryken, Leland. *The Liberated Imagination: Thinking Christianly About the Arts.* Wheaton, Ill.: Harold Shaw Publishers, 1989.

Sayers, Dorothy L. *The Mind of the Maker.* San Francisco: Harper Collins, 1987.

Schaeffer, Franky. *Addicted to Mediocrity: 20th Century Christians and the Arts.* Wheaton, Ill.: Crossway, 1981.

St. James, Elaine. *Living the Simple Life.* New York: Hyperion, 1996.

————. *Simplify Your Work Life.* New York: Hyperion, 2001.

Stoddard, Alexandra. *The Art of the Possible.* New York: Avon, 1995.

Thoreau, Henry David. *Walden and Other Writings, Introduction.* International Collectors Library. New York: Garden City, 1970.

Woolf, Virginia. *A Room of One's Own,* New York: Harcourt Brace Jovanovich, 1929, 1957.

Scripture Index

Subject Index

About the Author

Janice Elsheimer is a consultant and writer who specializes in helping people understand and nurture the creativity within themselves and others. She has taught creative writing and language arts for twenty-four years, from kindergarten through college level. She holds a master's degree in gifted education and works part-time as a teacher of gifted students. Janice has won awards for her poetry and essays, is a musician, and has other talents that are only just emerging. She practices her art in Winter Park, Florida, where she lives with her husband, Seth.